ANSWERING THE CALL

GISELLE WULFSOHN

The legacy of apartheid is tragically obvious throughout South Africa. Everywhere there are blatant disparities, conjured up by the architects of racial separation and entrenched until recently by many laws. Cities and towns brighten the night sky with megawatts of light, while candles and oil lamps flicker in neighbouring townships; four-lane highways sweep across the country while rutted dirt roads continue to serve millions of people. In 1994, a new South Africa was born and President Nelson Mandela stepped out to bring equal opportunity to all the peoples of South Africa, making them proud once more in their unity and strength.

Nowhere was the uneven distribution of services more apparent than in the basic human right to communicate. In sprawling but forgotten communities such as Sterkspruit in Transkei and Morokweng in Northern Province, a hundred thousand people would be served by one telephone line 30 kilometres away. While 98 per cent of the privileged had access to telephones, the average rate of telephone distribution dropped to one in a 100 in disadvantaged communities.

To prevent these massive backlogs in infrastructure from crippling the new democracy, business has had to harness foreign investment, be creative in its solutions and be passionate about improving the quality of life of the have-nots.

South African business is indeed fortunate to have a leader like President Nelson Mandela, who is able to radiate his vision for South Africa and its people so clearly that the goals are not only obvious, but desirable. It is an extraordinary feat that he has been able to achieve the same in the international business community.

As we have rolled up our sleeves to achieve these goals, the process of real economic empowerment has gathered momentum. In the cellular telephone industry alone, inroads have been made in wiping out the telecommunications backlog.

Cellular network operator Vodacom is playing a leading role in this process, helping to level the playing fields by providing cellular communications in disadvantaged areas. Hundreds of communities such as those at Sterkspruit and Morokweng have been boosted by the introduction of cellular community telephones. Scores of people have made their first phone call ever.

By June, 1997, three years after commercial operations started, the cellular industry had directly created more than 7 000 jobs, probably as many more jobs indirectly, and contributed more than R15 billion to the South African economy. The industry has also attracted substantial foreign investment.

It is expected that by June, 1999, the cellular industry's direct contribution to government revenue in the form of taxes, licence fees and additional income will exceed R8,8 billion.

A Joint Economic Development agreement with government saw the industry generating an additional R2 billion in economic activity outside its core business within three years.

There are, of course, many more examples of genuine private-public sector partnerships that have benefited the country. At the same time, we know there is still a long road ahead of us. It is the leadership of President Mandela that makes that road so clear to see.

This book is a celebration of that exceptional leadership and a country's transition from dark to light. Vodacom is proud to be associated with this tribute to President Mandela.

Alan Knott-Craig
Group Managing Director
Vodacom

Contents

Madiba

6 — *Foreword*
Archbishop Desmond Tutu believes that South Africa is extremely fortunate to have someone such as President Nelson Mandela at the helm of the country and concludes that he is, in every way, a special person.

8 — *Facets*
THE MARK OF THE MAN
The personality of Nelson Mandela is as many faceted as the diamonds given up by the soil of his native land. In an evocative series of vignettes *Shaun Johnson* throws light on some of the many sides that make up the President's scintillating persona.

20 — *Perspective*
THE MAKING OF A STATESMAN
The historical background to the life and times of the man who witnessed the rise and fall of apartheid and arguably helped more than any other to bring about its demise, recounted by *Steven Friedman*.

30 — *Freedom*
MANDELA IS COMING!
After close on three decades behind bars the world's most famous political prisoner steps on to the stage of a South Africa far different from the one he knew as a hunted and harried underground activist. *Ronald Morris* was there when Prisoner Number 466/64 became Nelson Mandela.

36 — *Communities*
A free and joyful *Madiba* loses no time in immersing himself in the country's many ethnic and religious communities to get his finger on the pulse of the nation he will soon lead to its democratic destiny.

44 — *Comrades*
Nelson Mandela has always stood by his friends and comrades through thick and thin and his name to them is a byword for staunchness. At an unusual reunion he gets together with some of the men who shared his island penal servitude.

50 — *Victors*
RETURN TO THE ISLAND
The sign over the prison entrance that greeted them in 1964 still says 'Welcome' as, four years to the day after his release from jail, Nelson Mandela returns with fellow convicts to Robben Island, where they revisit their old cells and the lime quarry where they toiled for nearly 13 years. *Michael Morris* recaptures this oddly nostalgic journey.

58 — *Transition*
THE DAWN OF DEMOCRACY
It was a time of frenzied comings and goings, of long, hard bargaining at the conference table, of accusation and counter–accusation, spirited confrontations and, finally, an inspired agreement that opened the doors to a new South Africa. *Kaizer Nyatsumba* recalls the at–times Byzantine convolutions of negotiations.

62 — *Elections*
FREEDOM AT LAST
Nelson Mandela leads his party on a campaign trail stomp that ends in April 1994 with nationwide democratic elections and, at the age of 76, he casts the first vote of his life in the country of his birth.

68 — *Inauguration*
The old flag comes down, FW de Klerk watches solemnly, and Nelson Mandela is sworn in at the Union Buildings, Pretoria, as the first South African democratically elected president.

Contents

70 *Integration*
The votes counted, the new president and his government installed, the time has come for integration at all levels of society — from parliament and the public service to the police force and the South African National Defence Force. President Mandela handles it all with adroit diplomacy.

72 *Crossroads*
WORLDS APART
One of the more intriguing little cameos of the transitional period in South Africa was the puzzling way in which what began as an apparently amicable association between FW de Klerk and Nelson Mandela gradually soured until they were worlds apart.

76 *Reconciliation*
BURYING THE PAST
This has been President Mandela's watchword since he assumed the mantle of leadership of the country's diverse and often deeply divided peoples. *Amina Cachalia* recounts what happened when he held out the olive branch to some of South Africa's more conservative citizens.

86 *Children*
THE YOUNG ONES
Nelson Mandela's love of children is deep and sincere. He says playing and chatting with them has always been one of the things that makes him feel at peace. One youngster will always remember the night the President came to his Barmitzvah and made him the envy of the Jewish community.

96 *Talisman*
THE MAGIC OF THE MAN
President Mandela has rightly seized upon sporting activity in a sports–mad country as the key to uniting all its peoples and the way he has done so has won the admiration of everyone in his rainbow nation, reports *Colin Bryden*.

106 *Style*
THE DRESSER & THE DANCER
The President is noted for his wardrobe of colourful casual shirts, which he dons for even the staidest of occasions. He is also known for his little soft shoe shuffle, which has been elevated to national status as the *Madiba* Dance.

112 *Spotlight*
HELLO WORLD
Men and women from all walks of life — kings and queens, presidents and politicians, pop stars and comedians — have been proud to stand beside the man who was born in a lowly hut in one of the country's poorest regions. *George Trail* relates how Nelson Mandela conquered the US and *Jim Penrith* charts his equally triumphant tours of Britain and his friendship with the Queen.

132 *Companions*
ONE FINE SPRING DAY
Abbey Makoe looks at the three women in Nelson Mandela's life who have claimed his love and respect, from his first wife Evelyn, who preferred religion to politics, second wife Winnie, the stormy petrel of the anti–apartheid struggle, and latterly Graca Machel, the widow of Mozambican President Samora Machel, who has joined him in the autumn of his life.

140 *Home*
HOME FROM HOME
All roads lead to home for President Mandela, whether it is the Transkei village of Qunu where he spent his early carefree years herding cattle and stick–fighting, or the elegant comfort of Genadendal, his official residence in Cape Town.

144 *Acknowledgements*
A word of appreciation to those who assisted the publishers.

⤙ Foreword

BENNY GOOL

SOMEONE SPECIAL

I first met Nelson Mandela in the 1950s when he was a rising lawyer and I was a student teacher. We went to debate against another school and Mandela adjudicated the contest. Even then he was cast as someone who would always be in the middle, weighing pros and cons and holding together divergent views, something like a judge. That was the last time I met him until his release from prison in 1990.

We corresponded often when he was in jail on Robben Island and I was Archbishop. After I received the Nobel Peace Prize in 1984, he wrote a letter saying the authorities had offered to release him provided he went to the Transkei. He responded with his usual verve by rejecting the offer with the disdain it deserved.

The next time I met *Madiba* was on February 11, 1990, after his release, when he came to stay at my official residence at Bishopscourt, Cape Town. Calls came from the White House and from all over the world to congratulate him. He was ever gracious, his old–world courtesy evident even then. He has the distinctive generosity of acknowledging everybody from the least to the highest, and saying thank you. He has a regal dignity but is quite humble, although he is also aware of status and position, and gives the respect due to high office.

I doubt whether *Madiba* has a mean bone in his entire make–up. His magnanimity is not laid on for special occasions. His altruistic gestures stem from a deep caring for people. Who else would have

⤙ 6   *Madiba*

Foreword

brought together the widows of political leaders from the former dispensation to a tea party? Who else would have thought of going to see Mrs Betsie Verwoerd, the widow of the prime architect of apartheid? Once these meetings had taken place we were not surprised, but who would have expected them to happen? He also strongly supported the Springbok as an emblem for the national rugby team, in spite of considerable opposition from his party. In effect, he was saying: this is the best way to approach the Afrikaner community, who must be feeling beleaguered, having lost power and feeling disorientated, with their world tumbling down.

Nobody could have carried this off with the panache that Mr Mandela did, walking on to the Ellis Park grounds in Johannesburg wearing the Number 6 jersey of the Springbok captain when South Africa won the 1995 Rugby World Cup. He had almost everybody eating out of his hand. He is quick to acknowledge the contribution of others, whereas mean spirited people are hypercritical and see the awful rather than the nice side of things. You can win people over more by praising what is good, rather than by clobbering them for what is wrong.

Mr Mandela showed his magnanimity when he dined with Dr Percy Yutar, the man who was prosecutor at the Rivonia Trial, which ended in June, 1964, with the jailing of the ANC's top leadership. Quite a few people were very surprised by this. This was the man who had put him behind bars for 27 years. But this magnanimity is not confined to *Madiba*. A rally was held in 1996, for the former treason trialists who wanted to say thank you to the South African Council of Churches for the support they were given at the time. Andy Young was there from the US. I was sitting next to Andy, and Andy was sitting next to Popo Molefe, who is today Premier of North West Province. On the other side was a white man, and Andy asked Popo who the man was. Popo replied, 'He is the judge who sentenced us.' Andy choked. When he addressed the group he asked, 'Can you imagine such a meeting in the Middle East or in Northern Ireland?' The judge was given gifts by the people he sent to jail!

We are extremely fortunate to have someone like *Madiba*. He is an icon representing national reconciliation when he says, let us forgive. He spent 27 years in jail. He speaks from a position of strength, with credibility. He has suffered.

Many people accept from him things that would be political suicide for any other politician to suggest. *Madiba* is someone special.

The Most Revd DM Tutu
Archbishop Emeritus and
Chairman of the Truth and Reconciliation Commission

↯ Facets

ARGUS

THE MARK OF
THE MAN

The story of Nelson Rolihlahla Mandela's life has been told many times over and from myriad points of view, from his birth on July 18, 1918, in the tiny rural village of Mvezo in the poverty–stricken Transkei, through his mission school days and his studies in Johannesburg to become a lawyer, to his political awakening and involvement in the African National Congress' struggle for liberation and his subsequent imprisonment on Robben Island and in a succession of other jails.

The world has been thrilled and enthralled by his emergence as a 20th century icon, a man who literally survived the slings and arrows of outrageous fortune to lead the land of his birth into a new era as South Africa's first democratically elected president.

While the major dates, places and turning points of this miraculous transition are well known, there have been smaller moments between the time of his release from prison and today; moments which give special insight to the many facets of this extraordinary man.

The following vignettes recorded by *Shaun Johnson* mark some particularly revealing moments in President Nelson Mandela's long and indelible walk across the African landscape.

↯ 8 *Madiba*

Facets

LS M BOWEY — SA NAVY

THE LEADER: *Soweto, 1990*

It is just a week since the most famous political prisoner in the world walked free through the gates of Victor Verster Prison, in Paarl, near Cape Town. Nelson Mandela is finally home, in the small Soweto house at number 8115 Vilakazi Street, Orlando West, that he last saw nearly three decades before. He sits in an unfamiliar suit in the cramped lounge; there are some of his old law books on the shelves.

He is still blinking in the bright world of freedom, surrounded by gadgetry he has never seen (a telephone answering machine, then state–of–the–art) but his mind is on politics, as ever. On Cape Town's Grand Parade seven days earlier, on an unforgettable evening, he delivered from text a carefully controlled, party–line address to mark his release so long in coming. Now, the formal encomiums and political homilies out of the way, he is ready to talk about the harsher reality of the fraught negotiations which lie ahead with a National Party government still very much in power. Some of his young activist aides are as fascinated as we are to hear the extempore, scriptless Mandela on strategy, and they crane to listen at the door. They are still shivering with the thrill of apparent revolutionary victory for the ANC, revolutionary defeat for the apartheid regime. But Mandela is not talking in triumphalist slogans. He is a team captain, leading, setting down markers to follower and foe alike about what is to come — and much of it will be unpalatable to those who owe him allegiance. He knows what must be done and he does it. At this extraordinarily early stage — there has been no formal meeting yet with government and Mandela's comrades are still in exile in Lusaka — he defines what will come to pass eventually at the Convention for a Democratic South Africa (Codesa).

'If you are not prepared to compromise,' he says loudly, 'then you must not enter into, or think about, the process of negotiation at all. Insignificant things, peripheral issues, don't need any compromise. You need to compromise on the fundamentals.' The message goes out to the world through the media, to the faithful through word of mouth. The settlement no one believed possible has taken its first firm step.

This is Nelson Mandela, the leader.

ABOVE: The cap fits, doffed by the Commander–in–Chief himself.

Madiba

Facets

HENNER FRANKENFELD/PICTURENET AFRICA

THE STOIC : *Stellenbosch, 1991*

It is an Autumn morning in the mountains near Stellenbosch, in the Western Cape. Nelson Mandela is sitting straight–backed in a Cape Dutch *voorkamer* and he is smiling through the pain etched like a canyon on his face. The tall man looks strangely smaller today, in spite of the ramrod bearing. Only 10 minutes earlier the telephone had brought once–unthinkable news: Winnie Mandela faces six years' imprisonment after being found guilty on charges of kidnapping and being an accessory to assault in the case of murdered child–activist Stompie Mokhetsi.

The most curious of countries, this. Barely a year after his release from prison, the African National Congress leader has just breached one of Afrikanerdom's intellectual citadels, mesmerising the students, and a few hours later he is in this strange room responding with unutterable dignity to the conviction of his wife by a white judge in the land of apartheid.

The room suffocates under the weight of the great unspoken question: will the pain of his situation cause Nelson Mandela to reject the court's verdict and, with it, the frighteningly fragile, nascent political negotiations? It was a time, which so many appear to have forgotten, when precious few believed those negotiations could survive. Finally the question comes: Have you now lost all confidence in the South African legal system? His voice is heavy but not querulous: 'Once an appeal has been made,' he says deliberately, 'it is proper to leave the matter in the hands of the court.'

'Proper' is a word Nelson Mandela uses more than most. A small sigh circulates around the room. He says later: 'The case itself has no direct relevance to negotiations.'

Then he tells a joke, and apologises to a local interviewer for his imperfect command of Afrikaans. The negotiating process has negotiated another moment of truth because he insists that the country's interests outweigh his own.

This is Nelson Mandela, the stoic.

THE SCOLDER : *Johannesburg, 1991*

It is Friday night, five days before Christmas in South Africa. The great first plenary session of the Convention for a Democratic South Africa (Codesa) is drawing to its scripted close. They are all here: the black president–in–waiting, the white president still in power, the pretenders, the horse–traders, the chancers, the ideologues and idealists, the technocrats, the curious. They are there to see the script go wrong for a heart–stopping half hour, though they don't know it yet.

On the podium, President FW de Klerk departs from the script which says he should close the historic armistice meeting with a message of optimism and generosity. The details are for history but the effect on Nelson Mandela is for this story. The normally kindly face of the septuagenarian leader clouds like a Johannesburg storm suddenly obliterating the blue dome of the highveld sky. The lieutenants nearest to him — Chris Hani and Joe Slovo — see it happen, and exchange urgent, worried glances.

As De Klerk closes, in the tone of a headmaster admonishing an errant pupil, it seems that a long shudder of anger passes through the ANC leader's body. Against his colleagues'

10   *Madiba*

Facets

GREG MARINOVICH/PICTURENET AFRICA

ROBBIE TSHABALALA

wishes, Nelson Mandela takes the stage slowly and with great deliberation. Nothing shakes but his fist. The cadence of his voice alters, assuming a quality which is close to a snarl. This is the steely side of the patriarch which few outside his inner circle have seen before.

He savages De Klerk: 'He does not represent us,' Mandela tells the audience and the world. 'He can't talk to us in that language.' It is a riveting spectacle. Nelson Mandela loses his temper when he perceives that his integrity or his dignity has been impugned. Many other than De Klerk — the ANC leadership itself and, most recently, representatives of the media who Mandela believes have behaved improperly — have had reason to remember this trait.

He views such slights as being aimed not so much at himself as his struggle, his party, his people.

There is not much — in the Codesa case not even the placatory efforts of the powerful Hanis and Slovos — which can stem the cold fury once unleashed.

It is true that he has the remarkable capacity of forgetting the firestorm once it has passed, and getting on with the business at hand. But history would be short–changed if this irascible characteristic was not recorded, in reality the side of the grandfatherly, beneficent personality which allows him to make the toughest of decisions and push them through to implementation.

This is Nelson Mandela, the scolder.

Madiba

↔ Facets

THE MODEST MAN
Washington, 1994

It is a triumphal tour by the leader of a relatively small African country to the most powerful nation in the world. The scale and enthusiasm of the welcome for Nelson Mandela shows that towering personalities can captivate the populace even of superpowers. President Mandela is meeting, among thousands of other important people, a hero of the Gulf War.

General Colin Powell, genuinely moved in the presence of the African giant, stretches out his hand and says: 'This is truly a very great honour for me.' President Mandela's response is quick, and delivered with the famous smile: 'No,' he says, 'it is a far greater honour for me. In fact, I won't wash this hand you have shaken.'

Countless others — ordinary and elevated alike — have experienced similar exchanges, and without exception have not suspected disingenuousness. It is one characteristic that no leader can learn in charm school; it is from the heart.

This is Nelson Mandela, the modest man.

Among the countless honours showered upon him by nations all over the world President Mandela particularly treasures the modest offering made in honour of his visit to world–famous Kirstenbosch National Botanical Garden, near Cape Town, in August, 1996.
This dazzling yellow strelitzia developed by curator John Winter has been renamed *Mandela's Gold*. Appropriately enough the flower, *Strelitzia reginae*, comes from the Eastern Cape, where the President was born. President Mandela's lifelong love of gardening was born at a mission school in Transkei, developed in the grim surroundings of Robben Island and nurtured at Pollsmoor Prison.

BENNY GOOL

BENNY GOOL

THE STATESMAN : *Johannesburg, 1992*

It is warm in Johannesburg's suburbia in the late afternoon sun as Nelson Mandela emerges from a solitary contemplative walk in the rose garden of his Houghton home. He is more relaxed than his countrymen, who are gripped by fury and fear. This is 1992, the mid–point of what would become South Africa's four year–long negotiated transition from minority rule to freedom. It is also the low point, the trough which followed the euphoric peak of release, unbanning and promise in 1990. There have been fresh, terrible massacres, the economy appears to be breaking down, the ANC has embarked on a campaign of 'rolling mass action' and — more than anything else the reason for the people's fear — the ANC has broken off all negotiations with the Pretoria government.

That negotiating process is still far from maturing to the point of irreversibility which will later see it survive the unspeakable killing of Chris Hani, the general secretary of the South African Communist Party. There is still overarching doubt at home and across the oceans that the racial Gordian Knot can be unravelled on the southern tip of Africa.

For the first (though not the last) time since Nelson Mandela's release, South Africans are realising that full–scale, Bosnian–style civil war is not an impossibility if the political leaders continue on their current course. Many among the battered, impatient black majority are prepared to counte-

Facets

nance this, so deep is the anger about Bisho, Boipatong and all the other bloodied battlefields.

If Nelson Mandela is to say now, today: There can be no settlement, we have been duped, it must be war, rise up — the people will rise and the clash with the still–intact government security forces and the as–yet unhumbled right wing will see the country slowly and savagely razed.

Mandela sees with stark strategic clarity what is at stake in this September month, and he is about to do what is unexpected but essential, and something that only he has the power and authority to do. It is his intention to dig deep into his own individual political capital and break the deadlock by sending an extraordinary message to the government.

Our country is sliding into anarchy, he says quietly, and only I and FW de Klerk can stop the slide; we must compromise, and compromise now. He then carefully sets out a series of steps which can be taken, and says he wants his organisation to return to the negotiating table.

He is keenly aware that this message, delivered softly in his living room, will resound like a thunderclap when it is publicised the next day.

He speaks poignantly, even avuncularly, about De Klerk, the man against whom he had launched such a devastating attack only months before. It is a metaphorical holding out of his hand, a gesture to be repeated famously and physically when the men debate on television prior to the election. 'I phoned him two days ago,' Nelson Mandela says, 'and I must say he sounded a bit down. He is a very brave chap, you know, very bright and confident, and it was worrying to hear him sounding so down.'

By the end of the next day, the conciliatory message having been delivered to the world, the national mood changes from deep despondency to renewed hope.

This is Nelson Mandela, the statesman.

14 *Madiba*

Facets

THE PATRIARCH
Maputo, 1994

TJ LEMON/PICTURENET AFRICA

It is dark in Maputo and the street is seething with noise and people. The people range from men in fine suits of Western and African style, to urchins in rags yelling their heads off in excitement. Cars are veering wildly, mounting the uneven sidewalks. The pedestrians have taken over the road and the traffic will not be able to reclaim it for some time. Some motorists jump out of their vehicles to join the swelling crowd, original errands forgotten, keys left in the ignition.

Everyone, irrespective of social station, is jostling for position and the aim is the same — to get as close as possible to the tall man in front, striding ahead of the throng looking for all the world like the Pied Piper of Africa. He is enjoying himself enormously, touching hands and patting heads.

Nelson Mandela is in town, and the town has never seen anything like it.

In the joyous, chaotic stampede, small scenes say so much: Robert Mugabe is practically pushed out of the way by four determined youths who don't even look at him long enough to recognise the president of Zimbabwe. They are making the best of their one chance to walk with *Madiba*.

President Joachim Chissano, though he is the host, is temporarily separated from his famous guest as the people unthreateningly but insistently circumvent the security arrangements. Mobutu Sese Seko, president of Zaire, tags along dolefully some way behind, as do several other African potentates, unused to the completeness of the overshadowing.

The scene at the leaders' summit in Mozambique is an especially vivid illustration of Nelson Mandela's standing as patriarch of Africa, but it has been replicated innumerable times elsewhere on the continent and in the capitals of the world. It is the kind of event which will convince future historians to accord to the South African deliverer a millennial significance comparable to that of the likes of Mahatma Gandhi.

Mandela is, even while still in office, assured of his status as one of the greatest figures of the 20th century.

This is Nelson Mandela, the African patriarch.

Madiba 15

⤱ Facets

LOUISE GUBB/i-AFRIKA

THE COMPASSIONATE : *Western Cape, 1996*

It is *a boiling, dusty, harsh afternoon* at Elim, the quaint Western Cape village which has grown up around the old mission station in the hinterland of the Overberg. The day of campaigning for the 1996 local elections has already been long for President Mandela, dressed reluctantly in a dark suit because the old-fashioned, isolated community might take a '*Madiba* shirt' amiss. The schedule has gone wildly awry, the air force helicopter is waiting, and an exhausted President Mandela must still fly back to Cape Town and without a break rush to address a public meeting in the heart of the city's white southern suburbs. But the children at the small local hospital, terribly afflicted children, have been promised that he will visit.

Madiba's harassed aides know that he will not be persuaded to disappoint them.

In the most tragic of all the wards, pandemonium breaks out as the large entourage enters and the children run helter-skelter among the dignitaries, the aides, the security men, the journalists. President Mandela is but one figure in the crush, in spite of his height, and the children could be forgiven for not knowing where to focus their attention. But here we enter the realms of aura and of instinct: they are drawn to the source of dignified warmth in the melee, though he has not spoken a word. One girl, her limbs achingly deformed, slides across the floor, grabs at the President's trouser cuff, and hangs on for dear life.

Facets

LOUISE GUBB/i-AFRIKA

Politicians throughout history and around the world know that children are vote–catchers, but no one who knows Nelson Mandela doubts that he loves them and they feel it.

Some of his most emotional reactions to tragic situations have been sparked by the suffering of children — it was so at Swanieville, at Boipatong, and so many other places — but it is a thread of his personality which is not widely understood, but should be, given his 27 years of imprisonment without the company of children.

This is Nelson Mandela, the compassionate.

LOUISE GUBB/i-AFRIKA

ABOVE AND LEFT: A soft spot for all children... Nelson Mandela gets his nose tweaked by his grandson, Bhambhata on his first trip back to Qunu in Transkei during May, 1990.

Madiba 17

THE SOLITARY MAN
Johannesburg, 1994

It is only a matter of days before Nelson Mandela's people will go to the polls and begin the final dismantling of apartheid, vote by vote. The negotiations are over and the new society shimmers on the horizon.

One would not immediately feel the weight of the moment, just to look at him in his home on this Saturday morning before the most decisive week in South Africa's history. But the weight is there, pressing down.

The president–in–waiting wears light linen slip–on shoes and a characteristically fashionable red shirt hanging open casually around the waist. He graciously offers tea and begins a long, profound discussion about the events to come, the grave risks and the heart–soaring possibilities for his country and all its people.

It is a big home he is living in now, though unexceptional by the standards of affluent Johannesburg. But there is an inescapable air in this house, in its hallways and anterooms and on its staircases.

The world's most admired man — and, in this historic period, the world's most sought–after interviewee — looks lonely behind his smile. He is surrounded by people, but they do not live with him: he will retire tonight alone with his thoughts.

He is asked whether, at these extraordinary crossroads in his history and that of the country, the continent, the world, he harbours

SASA KRALJ/i–AFRIKA

Facets

any regrets about the route his life has taken. He thinks for a long time before answering.

'I hope I would do the same over again,' he says, 'though it has not been easy. To see your family, your children being persecuted when you are absolutely helpless in jail, that is one of the most bitter experiences, most painful experiences, I have had. Your wife being hounded from job to job, your children being taken out of schools, police breaking into your house at midnight and even assaulting your wife ...'

He is in a reverie now, talking to himself as much as his questioner. 'So I have wondered sometimes whether I have made the correct decisions. I had not anticipated the repression in relation to my family... But at the end of the agonising I felt, no, it was correct. My commitment was proper.'

There is little more to say, and the audience is over. Except, that is, for a thought that brings the smile back to his face: 'This is going to be our greatest moment, you know,' he beams, 'April, 27.'

As we leave the house the Old Man is smiling, and he waves. But a backward glance sees him then become as still and calm as a statue. This is Nelson Mandela, the solitary man.

But the scene has been overtaken. Unpredictable, occasionally kind fate has provided an uplifting footnote. Though he lived through the greatest sea change in his country's history with no partner at his side, he is not destined to be alone forever, as pictures in this book of the President and his new companion, Graca Machel, testify. — SHAUN JOHNSON, GROUP EDITORIAL DIRECTOR, INDEPENDENT NEWSPAPERS OF SOUTH AFRICA.

NAASHON ZALK/PICTURENET AFRICA

The solitary man no more. President Mandela in a characteristic pose with the new lady in his life, Graca Machel, widow of Mozambican president Samora Machel. Their joy is there for all to see but both have publicly announced that there will be no wedding bells.

Madiba 19

✣ Perspective

THE MAKING OF A STATESMAN

Right: Nelson Mandela in the traditional Xhosa dress he wore in court in 1962, when he was sentenced to five years in jail for inciting workers to strike and leaving the country without valid travel documents.

Opposite: The *rondavel* in Mqhekezweni, 'the Great Place', in Thembuland where Nelson Mandela lived from the age of nine, after his father died, and where the Thembu Regent, Jongintaba, became his guardian and mentor.

ELI WEINBERG/IDAF, LONDON

✣ 20 *Madiba*

Perspective

$\mathcal{T}$he political life of Nelson Mandela is woven into the most dramatic tale in South African history: the rise and fall of apartheid. He has shaped that story, just as it has shaped him. The story begins in the latter years of World War II, a time of intellectual ferment in the colonised world.

MAYIBUYE CENTRE

Madiba

Perspective

MAYIBUYE CENTRE

ABOVE: Nelson Mandela at the age of 19 in one of his earliest known photographs.

OPPOSITE TOP: Mandela in the office of the law practice he and Oliver Tambo opened in 1952, in central Johannesburg, the first black practice in the city. Nelson Mandela was the only black student at the Law School of the University of the Witwatersrand in Johannesburg in the mid–1940s.

OPPOSITE BOTTOM: The Wits University Law Class of '46 with Nelson Mandela (back row, second left) and as they are today. (BACK ROW, FROM LEFT): Richard Ascham, Johann Moller, David John, Adv Philip Wulfsohn SC, Charl Cilliers, Harry Schwarz, Judge Henry Preiss, Adv George Bizos SC. CENTRE ROW: Adv Stephen Rein, Prof Ellison Kahn, Sidney Bloch, Henry Nathanson, Adv Jules Browde, Ahmed Bhoola, Judge Nic Nicholas. FRONT ROW: Lionel Benjamin, Bomber Wells, President Nelson Mandela, Nathan Lochoff, Max Levenberg.

Democracy's battle against fascism inspired African and Asian thinkers, inviting comparisons between the stated Allied commitment to democracy and the denial of freedom to European colonies. Like their counterparts elsewhere, the intellectuals and professionals who formed the African National Congress Youth League in 1944 — the youthful Mandela among them — believed it possible and necessary to demand in their countries what was being won in Europe. They urged a militant campaign against white supremacy — an end to the ANC tactic of dignified moral argument by a small educated elite.

Mandela, then one of the country's few black lawyers, was particularly wedded, he was later to recall, to a militancy which stressed that black Africans could win freedom only if they rejected co–operation with other races. Freedom seemed a more likely prospect then than it would for much of the next four decades.

While black people were victims of legalised discrimination in the 1940s, apartheid was only an idea in the mind of the National Party, then the Opposition in the white parliament. It seemed plausible that peaceful mass resistance might win for the black majority full political rights. The next decade and a half were indeed to see the militant resistance which the Youth League championed, but it also saw, after the National Party's 1948 electoral victory, the hardening of a comprehensive system of racial domination.

The architects of rigid race segregation set to work with a will in 1950, legislating the Group Areas Act, mandating residential racial separation, the Population Registration Act, establishing an elaborate system of race classification, and the Immorality Act, outlawing inter–racial sex (marriage across the racial divide was barred by the 1949 Mixed Marriages Act).

22 *Madiba*

Perspective

JÜRGEN SCHADEBERG

WITS UNIVERSITY/PICTURENET AFRICA

THOMAS CHAUKE/MARKET PHOTOGRAPHY WORKSHOP

Madiba

Perspective

JÜRGEN SCHADEBERG/BAILEY'S AFRICAN PHOTO ARCHIVES

On June 26, 1952, the ANC launched its Defiance of Unjust Laws campaign throughout South Africa, in collaboration with the Indian Congress. Jails were filled to overflowing with blacks and Indians who volunteered to break targeted laws, often informing police and magistrates of their intention beforehand. Nelson Mandela, (above) with activist Ruth First, was the National Volunteer in Chief of the campaign.

RIGHT: Mandela hands a letter to a magistrate informing him that volunteers will be breaking the pass laws in his area.

COURTESY: AMINA CACHALIA

The Suppression of Communism Act of that year banned the South African Communist Party but also provided the government with a weapon against all opposition to apartheid. Other measures followed: laws in 1952 and 1957 tightened influx control, making it more difficult for black people to live and work in the cities. In 1953, the Separate Amenities Act imposed segregation on all public facilities.

As apartheid tightened its grip, the ANC, guided by a programme devised by the Youth League, mobilised non–violent resistance designed to build a mass anti–apartheid movement. The most celebrated action of the decade was the 1952 Defiance Campaign, in which volunteers defied apartheid laws, courting arrest by first notifying the authorities that they were about to do so. It was followed by campaigns against segregated education and forced removals of black people from areas now designated 'white', bus boycotts and mass work stay–aways.

Mandela played a pivotal role in the resistance: he was a key Defiance Campaign organiser and rose to become Transvaal president and first deputy president of the ANC. While he became increasingly willing to work with white and Indian activists, his commitment to militancy remained unchanged.

He soon acquired a reputation as an organiser and strategist. In the former role, he travelled across the country, seeking to organise resistance and build ANC support. In the latter, he devised the 'M Plan', a strategy of tight grassroots organisation designed to protect the movement against the anticipated government ban. While it was not implemented effectively at the time, it was to influence township resistance during the 1980s.

The new militancy was non–violent. It remained an ANC article of faith that apartheid could be ended by peaceful

Perspective

BAILEY'S AFRICAN HISTORY ARCHIVES

JÜRGEN SCHADEBERG

BOB GOSANI/BAILEY'S AFRICAN PHOTO ARCHIVES

TOP LEFT: After the government introduced the Bantu Education Act, which Dr Hendrik Verwoerd, the minister responsible for its implementation in 1955, declared would 'train and teach people in accordance with their opportunities in life', the ANC launched a boycott of government schools which saw Mandela doing the rounds to stiffen resistance to apartheid education.

TOP RIGHT: Discussing his case with colleagues outside the Transvaal Supreme Court after one of his many brushes with the law.

LEFT: Delegates from all over South Africa gather at Kliptown, near Johannesburg, in June, 1955, for a Congress of the People to approve the ANC's Freedom Charter, a revolutionary document that became a beacon for the liberation struggle.

Madiba 25

Perspective

RIGHT: Dr Yusuf Dadoo, president of the South African Indian Congress, with Nelson Mandela.

COURTESY: AMINA CACHALIA

BELOW: Nelson Mandela talks to some of the anti–pass protesters who defied the law and went to jail in their hundreds.

PETER MAGUBANE/BAILEY'S AFRICAN HISTORY ARCHIVES

mobilisation. But the fight against the apartheid state was then an unequal one. None of the resistance's aims was achieved and the government used its legislative battery to curb both resistance and resisters.

Mandela was a key victim. He was banned — prohibited from political activity or from mixing with more than one person at a time (he was, he later recalled, formally barred from attending his son's birthday party) — imprisoned and then prosecuted in the Treason Trial of the 1950s, a legal marathon in which ANC leaders spent, in many cases, years in court before they were acquitted of high treason.

The acquittal was a pyrrhic victory. It came, in March, 1961, a year after the Sharpeville massacre and its aftermath: a State of Emergency and the banning of the ANC and other resistance organisations. Mandela and his colleagues might be nominally free, but the organisation they led was no longer allowed to operate.

Sharpeville seemed to confirm what some in the ANC had begun to suspect through the 1950s: that the system was too strong, the government too ruthless to allow peaceful, legal, change. It was also a heady period, one in which many South Africans were convinced that apartheid's overthrow was nigh. In reality, it began the 'Silent Sixties', a period in which resistance was muzzled and apartheid continued its seemingly inexorable march to supremacy.

Immediately after the trial, Mandela disappeared underground to organise ANC clandestine resistance. He travelled about

26 *Madiba*

Perspective

LEFT: Police atop armoured vehicles watch as people gather for an anti–pass demonstration at a black township whose name would soon claim headlines around the world.

BELOW: The massacre, in March, 1960, that wrote the name Sharpeville in blood. The scene after police opened fire on the protesters, killing 69. Mandela said that after Sharpeville South Africa was a different place.

the country disguised as a chauffeur or labourer, constituting secret ANC branches and mobilising resistance.

For 17 months, dubbed 'The Black Pimpernel' by the press, he evaded arrest.

For a while, the ANC remained committed to non–violence. Mandela had first discussed armed resistance in 1952. He had, he later declared, become convinced of its necessity after the Sophiatown removals of 1955. After lengthy discussion, he persuaded the underground ANC to endorse armed struggle. At his insistence, the ANC leadership agreed to the formation, under his leadership, of *Umkhonto weSizwe* (MK), the 'Spear of the Nation', a rudimentary guerrilla army.

In August, 1962, after his return from a trip through Africa to drum up support for MK, Mandela was arrested near Pietermaritzburg. In November, 1962, he was sentenced to five years in prison for political offences.

Eleven months into his sentence, he was on trial for his life after the police arrested the MK High Command at *Lilliesleaf* Farm, in the Johannesburg suburb of Rivonia. To the relief of many ANC supporters — who had expected Mandela and his co–accused to hang — they were sentenced to life in prison. Throughout this period, the rigidity of apartheid, and the severity and efficiency of the government which presided over it, made the system seem immune to challenge.

Mandela's circumstances seemed to confirm this. For the next 26 years, he remained in prison. For two decades, he was a political spectator, his role limited

Madiba

⤝ Perspective

PETER MAGUBANE/BAILEY'S AFRICAN PHOTO ARCHIVES

TIMES MEDIA LTD/MUSEUM AFRICA

to that of symbol of resistance and influence over scores of activists who encountered him at the Robben Island prison cells. In the first of these decades, the system he was pledged to fight continued to strengthen: ever–harsher security laws buttressed apartheid, which was ever more strictly applied.

More than 11 500 people were convicted under the Immorality Act before its repeal in the 1980s; by 1975, more than 540 000 a year fell foul of influx control; by the mid–1970s, 459 000 people had been removed from their homes by the Group Areas Act.

The system which had, a few years earlier, appeared set to end in a revolutionary convulsion seemed likely to last well beyond the lifetime of the imprisoned symbol of resistance. But in 1973, the resistance Mandela championed re–emerged when black workers in Durban struck for higher pay. Three years later, pupils in Soweto rebelled against Afrikaans–medium education. Resistance grew in the 1980s, culminating in the violent township conflicts of 1984, and beyond.

The resistance, and apartheid's growing unworkability, posed the first substantial threat to the system since its introduction. In 1985, the government again declared an Emergency, at first a partial one and then, the next year, one covering the entire coun-

TOP: Mandela comes in from the rain to make a dramatic appearance at a conference in Pietermaritzburg while operating underground, one of the surprise visits that earned him the name 'The Black Pimpernel'. He was subsequently arrested near Pietermaritzburg, which 25 years later conferred on him the Freedom of the City.

LEFT: Nelson Mandela and some of the accused in the marathon treason trial relax during a break in proceedings.

⤝ 28 *Madiba*

Perspective

try. The purpose now was not to ensure permanent black quiescence; the white political establishment had accepted that apartheid could not endure.

The Emergency aimed to control change, not to end it. And, unlike the earlier decree, it failed. The events of the mid–1980s were to culminate not in the modified white rule for which the government hoped, but in universal franchise. Mandela played a pivotal role in ensuring this. By 1985 he, too, had concluded that apartheid might end, and that its demise might be hastened.

A negotiated way to majority rule, the ANC hope of the pre–Youth League period, seemed possible. In changed circumstances, the wheel had turned full circle. In 1985, Mandela wrote to Justice Minister Kobie Coetsee, suggesting talks between the ANC and the government. Gradually, the government responded.

By 1987, Mandela was engaged in talks with the establishment which had once seemed likely to hang him. The process was to end in the non–racial poll of 1994, and Mandela's election as president.

The militant who had, with his angry young colleagues of the 1940s, begun to mobilise resistance to apartheid had become the statesmen who would negotiate its end. — *Steven Friedman, Director, Centre for Policy Studies, Johannesburg.*

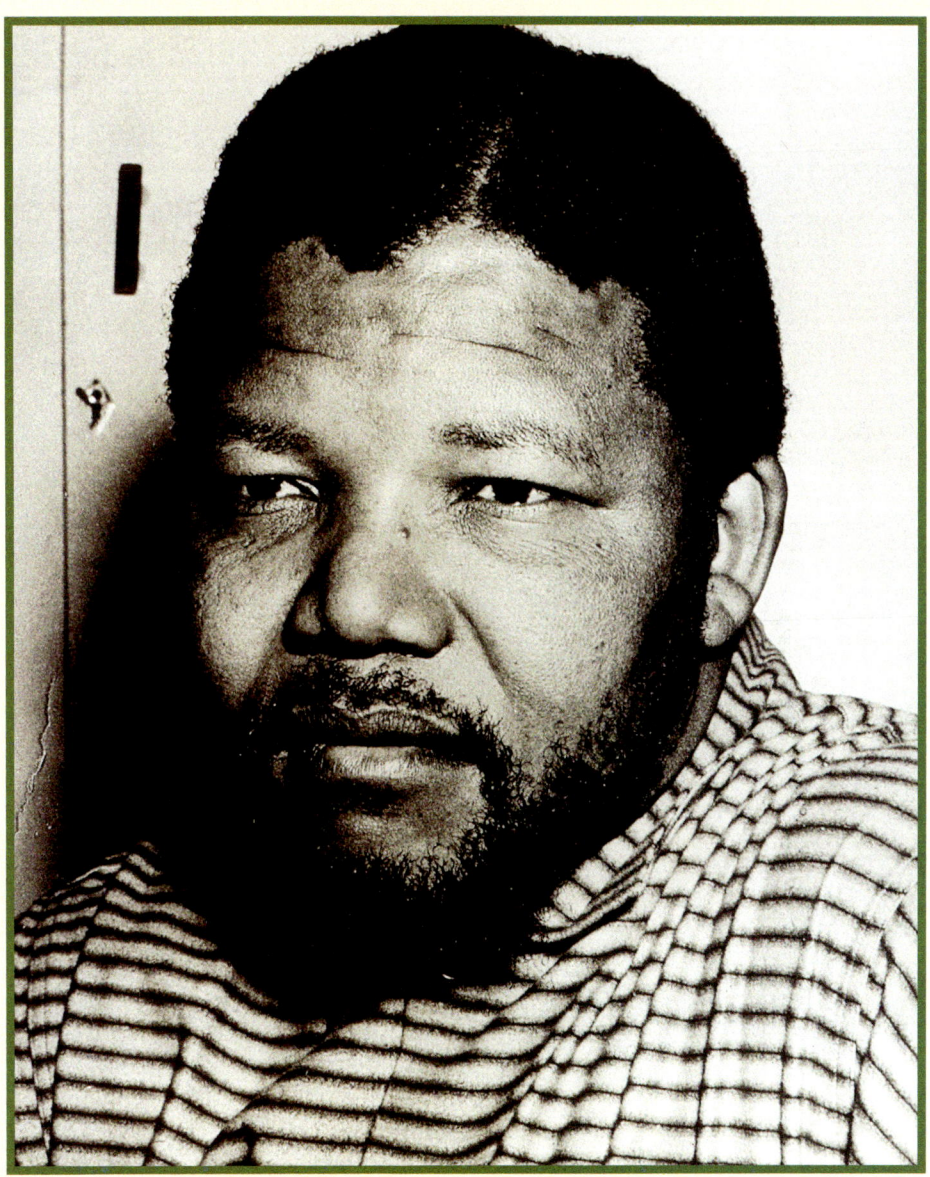
COURTESY: AFRICAN NATIONAL CONGRESS ARCHIVES

Top: A bearded Mandela as he was during the two years he spent underground.

PETER MAGUBANE/BAILEY'S AFRICAN PHOTO ARCHIVES

Right: Undaunted treason trialists give the ANC thumbs–up sign from the barred windows of a *kwela–kwela* – police van – as they arrive at court in Johannesburg in 1957.

Madiba 29

COURTESY: AFRICAN NATIONAL CONGRESS ARCHIVES/THE STAR

ABOVE: A poster makes an important proclamation as four eager children await the return to Soweto of the man who last saw his house in Orlando West nearly 30 years earlier. The photograph appears in an album presented to President Mandela by *The Star,* Johannesburg.

At 4.16pm on February 11, 1990, Prisoner Number 466/64 walked out of the grounds of Victor Verster Prison, near Paarl, and became once more Nelson Mandela, a free man after spending 27 years in jail for his opposition to apartheid. Journalists from all over the world were among the first people to gather outside the prison gates as morning broke. Police and army roadblocks were set up on roads leading to the prison, obliging the multitude of supporters and well–wishers to walk there while armed prison guards stood watch at regular intervals at the waist–high roadside fence.

A beaming Nelson Mandela emerged to ecstatic cheers and applause from the thousands of people who had waited under a blazing sun since dawn to welcome him. Hand–in–hand with his then wife Winnie and flanked by African National Congress (ANC) stalwart Cyril Ramaphosa, the world's most famous prisoner walked the short distance to the prison gates and waved to the crowd.

30 *Madiba*

Freedom

COURTESY: SOUTH AFRICAN COMMUNICATION SERVICES

LEFT: One of the first pictures of Nelson Mandela to be published in South Africa since 1964 and, for many South Africans, their first view of the man destined to be their President. It was taken on February 9, 1990, when he met then President FW de Klerk in Cape Town two days before his release from prison.

Madiba

Freedom

The thin blue line of policemen spread across the road wavered and ANC marshals battled to control a near–hysterical crowd which surged forward while photographers and television crews scrambled to capture the first pictures of a free Nelson Mandela. Several helicopters carrying media representatives hovered nearby, prevented by strict security laws from overflying the prison. One enterprising foreign television cameraman paid a Cape Town City Council hoist–truck driver to park his vehicle outside the prison gates with the platform raised so that he could get a bird's–eye view of the unfolding drama.

Thousands of ANC supporters, many waving the black, green and gold flag of the party, chanted and sang and mobbed Mandela's car before it was shepherded away by motorcycles at the head of a convoy of vehicles carrying the leadership of the Mass Democratic Movement. As the motorcade sped off to Cape Town, thousands of people of all races lined the route, hoping for a glimpse of the man who had become a legend in his own lifetime.

TIMES MEDIA LTD/BRIAN HENDLER

On Cape Town's historic Grand Parade an estimated quarter of a million people had waited in the summer heat for up to 12 hours to hear Mandela speak. By the time he finally appeared on the balcony of the City Hall the crowd, which had dwindled to about 50 000, exploded into roars of *Amandla* and *Viva* and near–hysterical screaming. There was an expectant silence as Mandela spoke his first words to a South African crowd in nearly three decades: 'Friends, comrades and fellow South Africans, I greet you in the name of peace, and democracy for all. I stand here before you not as a prophet, but as a humble servant of you, the people. Your tireless and heroic sacrifices have made it possible for me to be here today. I therefore place the remaining years of my life in your hands.'

His 20–minute speech contained no deviation from ANC policy positions. He called for the intensification of the freedom struggle, including armed resistance, defiance and the international isolation of the apartheid regime. He did, however, strike a conciliatory note by acknowledging that then President FW de Klerk had taken 'real steps to normalise the situation' and called on 'our white compatriots to join us in the shaping of the new South Africa'.

Then the crowd sang *Nkosi Sikelel' iAfrika* — 'God Bless Africa'. With that, Nelson Mandela went out into the country to meet his people. — RONALD MORRIS, SENIOR WRITER, THE CAPE TIMES

ABOVE: The poster that says it all.

RIGHT: The picture that flashed around the world on February 11, 1990. Nelson Mandela takes his first steps to freedom with his then wife, Winnie, out of the gates of Victor Verster Prison, in the Western Cape winelands town of Paarl. This is the moment that ended nearly three decades of imprisonment for the man who became the world's most famous convict.

Freedom

CAPE ARGUS/i-AFRIKA

Madiba 33

⊱ Freedom

RIGHT: Nelson Mandela embraces his tearful relative, pop star Brenda Fassie, at his home in Orlando West, near Johannesburg, after his release from prison.

BELOW: Basking in freedom at Bishopscourt, Cape Town, with comrades old and new.

LOUISE GUBB/I-AFRIKA

WALTER DHLADLA

34   *Madiba*

LOUISE GUBB/i-AFRIKA

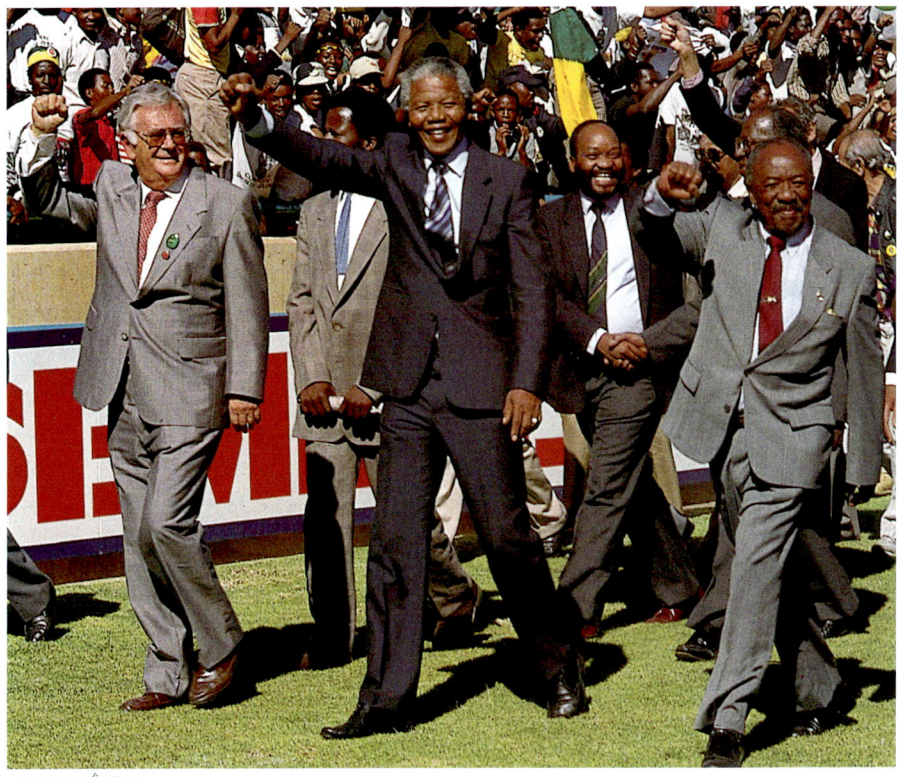

LEFT: Nelson Mandela marches into a Soweto stadium to address his first political rally in more than 30 years.

BELOW: Township children flock to welcome Nelson Mandela as he returns to the home in Soweto he last saw nearly 30 years ago.

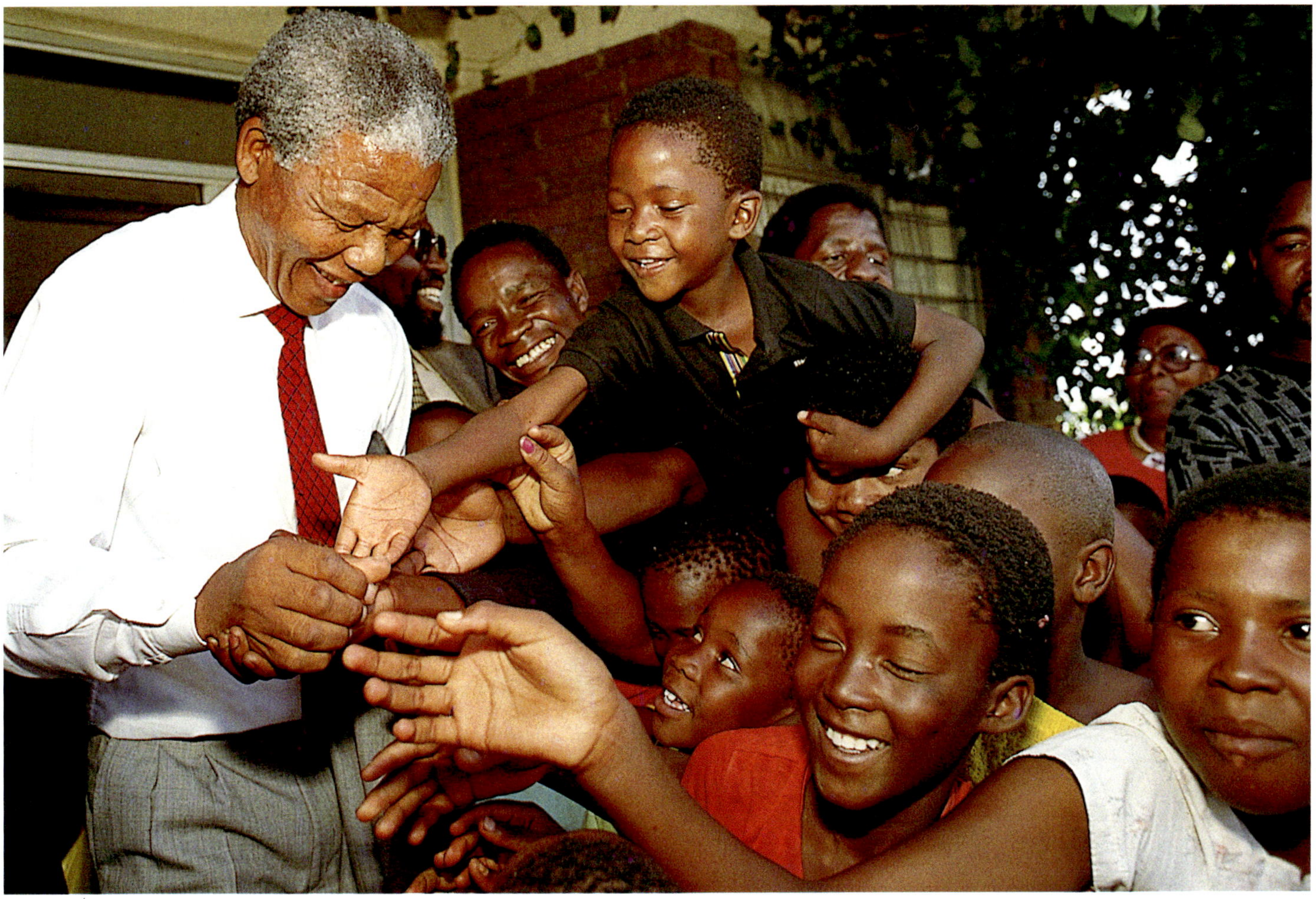

LOUISE GUBB/i-AFRIKA

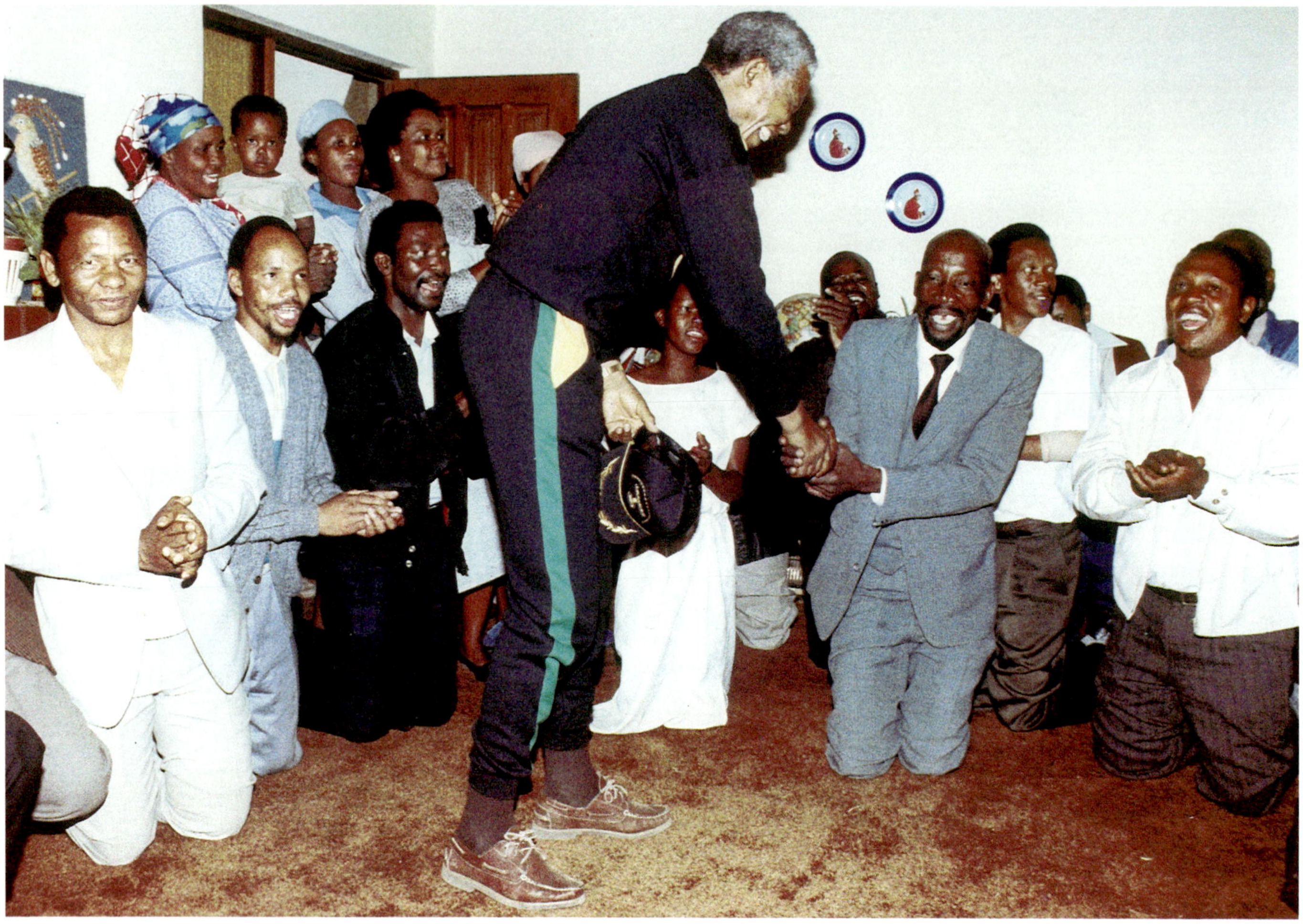

WALTER DHLADLA

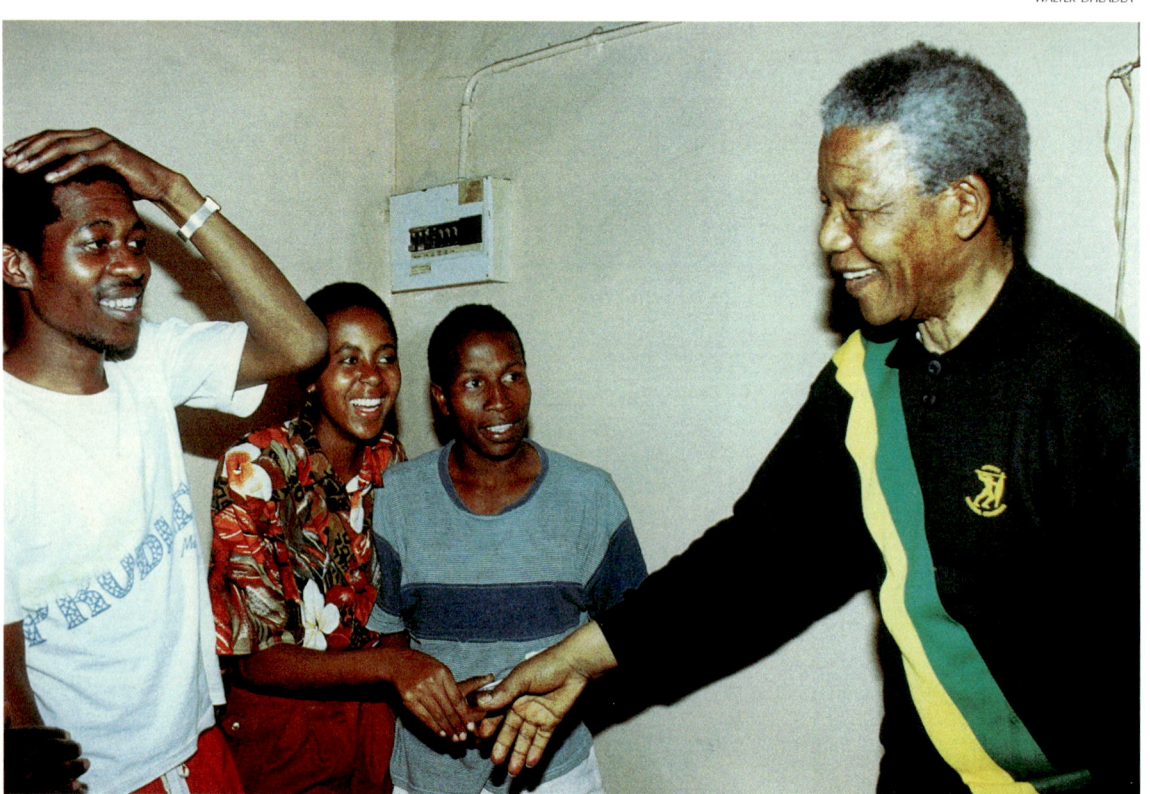

After his release from prison, Nelson Mandela went out to meet South Africa's communities.

THESE PAGES: Mandela's walkabout to meet the people elicits traditional greetings from delighted friends and supporters and ends with an impromptu dance performed by an elated elder as Mandela claps along with onlookers.

WALTER DHLADLA

Communities

Madiba

WALTER DHLADLA

⚹ Communities

RIGHT: President Mandela shows keen interest in Afrikaner relics on display at the Huguenot Museum in Franschhoek, Western Cape.

BELOW: In Cape Town on the election trail in 1993, Nelson Mandela took time out to sing *Nkosi Sikelel' iAfrika* with the Catholic community.

OPPOSITE: No form of transport is too humble for this popular Head of State. President Mandela rides a local donkey cart to attend third anniversary election celebrations at Upington, in the Northern Cape Province.

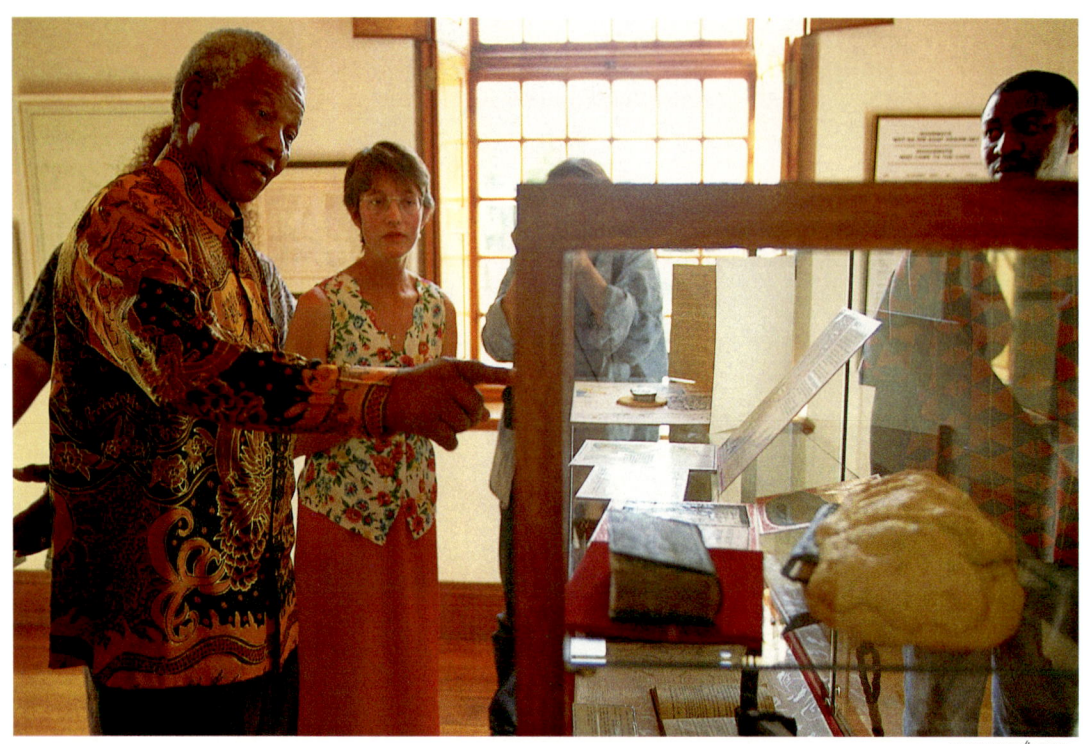

LOUISE GUBB/i-AFRIKA

LOUISE GUBB/i-AFRIKA

⚹ 38 *Madiba*

RIGHT: LOUISE GUBB/i-AFRIKA

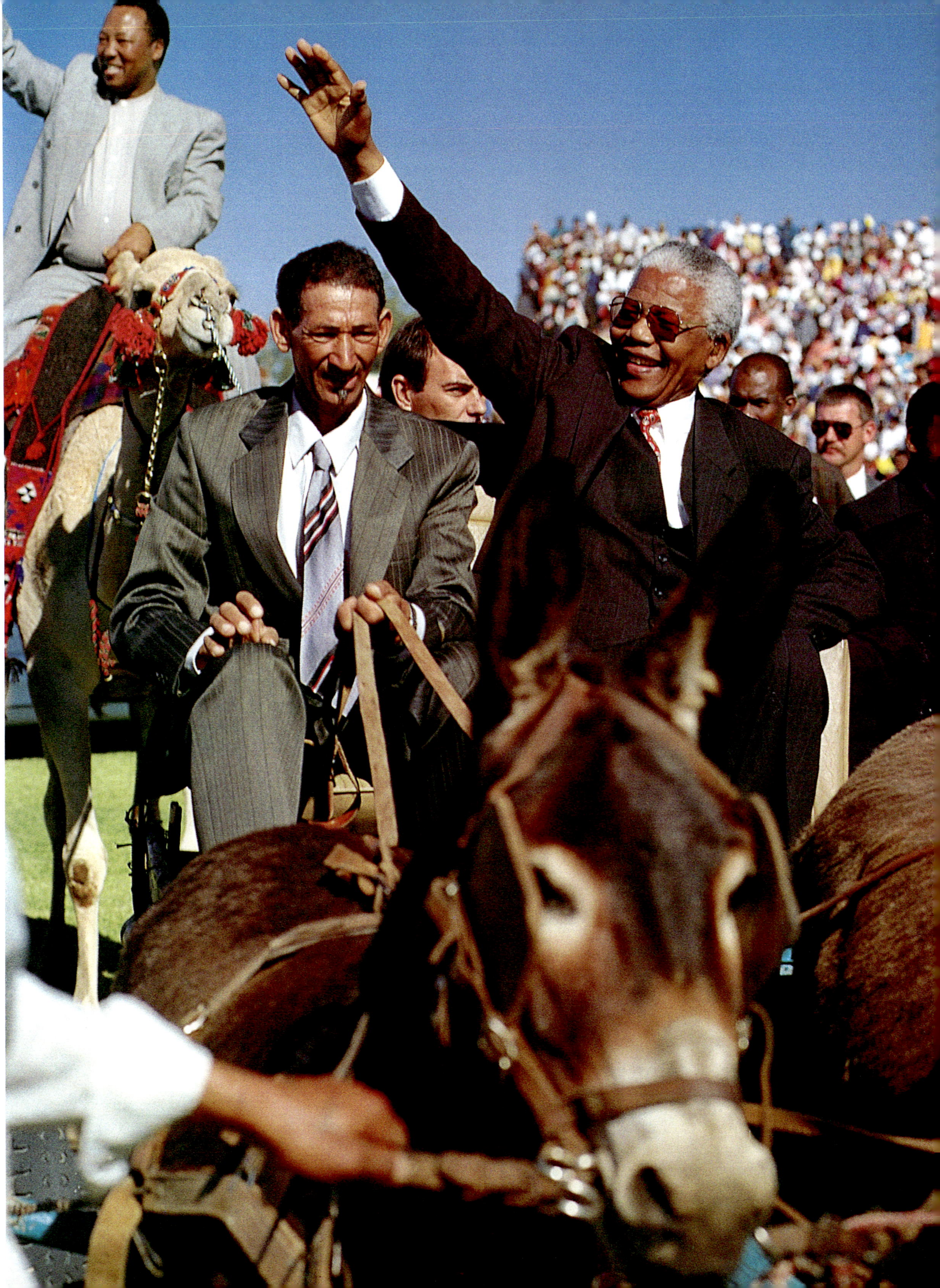

⁌ Communities

RODGER BOSCH/i-AFRIKA

⁌ 40   Madiba

Communities

OPPOSITE: Continuing his journey to meet all communities in the country, Nelson Mandela visits a mosque.

ABOVE LEFT: He pays his respects to Cyril Harris, Chief Rabbi of the Union of Orthodox Synagogues in South Africa. Mandela retains special links with the South African Jewish community and often recalls that it was members of their legal fraternity that came to his aid during the years he and other ANC leaders were in and out of court and no one else wanted to be associated with men widely regarded as terrorists.

ABOVE RIGHT: Nelson Mandela opens the Anne Frank exhibition in Johannesburg in 1994, recalling that he and other prisoners derived encouragement from reading the little Jewish girl's wartime diary while they were on Robben Island. 'Heroines of Anne's calibre kept our spirits high and reinforced our confidence in the invincibility of the cause of freedom and justice,' he said, praising the Anne Frank Foundation for its consistent stand against fascism and apartheid.

Madiba

❧ Communities

RIGHT: No sections of the community are ignored as Madiba embraces all, among them a nurse during his visit to a hospital in Gauteng province.

BELOW: Years of wielding a pick and shovel in a prison quarry give President Mandela a practised hand when it comes to turning the first sod at a Reconstruction and Development Programme water scheme in the North West Province.

OPPOSITE, TOP: Now it's the turn of the performing arts as Madiba meets actors in the Zulu version of *Macbeth* and (below) he meets members of the Indian community in Lenasia, near Johannesburg.

BENNY GOOL/SOUTHERN IMAGES

LOUISE GUBB/i-AFRIKA

Madiba

Communities

HENNER FRANKENFELD/PICTURENET AFRICA

HENNER FRANKENFELD/PICTURENET AFRICA

Madiba

Comrades

Comrades

REUNION

Nelson Mandela prides himself on never letting down a friend and has gone to extraordinary lengths to keep in touch with old comrades and their families. Among the many, Oliver Tambo was the closest friend and comrade Nelson Mandela ever had. They first met as students at the missionary–run University College of Fort Hare, where the young Mandela admired Tambo's diamond–edged intelligence. Their lives became inextricably bound; they set up a law office together in Johannesburg, they plunged into struggle politics together, they were arraigned in the treason trial, they helped to shape the ANC. The bonds of friendship remained unshakeable even after Tambo left the country in 1960 to represent the ANC in exile and Mandela began his long term of imprisonment.

Madiba

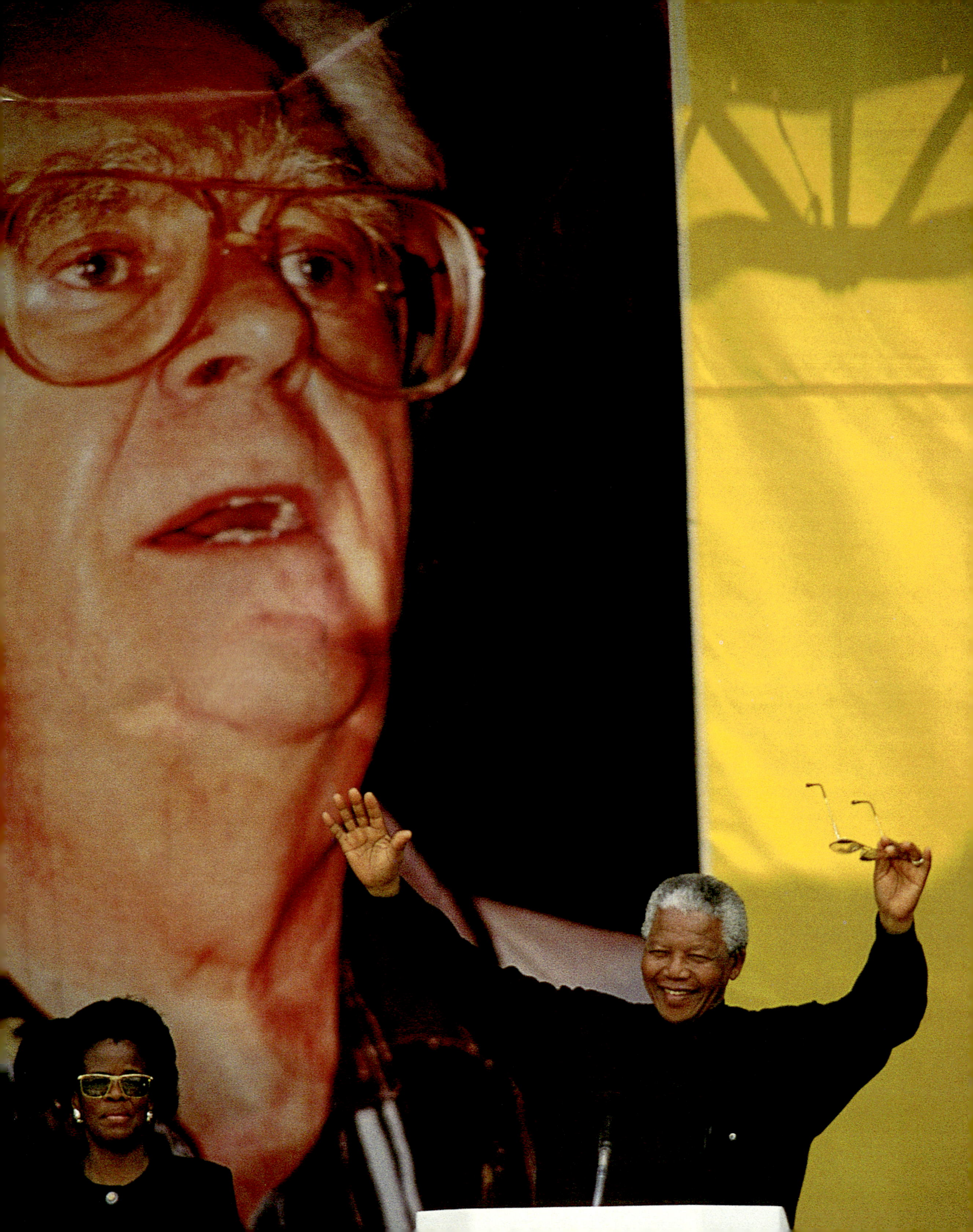

Comrades

PAUL VELASCO/PICTURENET AFRICA

PREVIOUS PAGES, LEFT: Nelson and Winnie Mandela at a celebratory supper with Oliver and Adelaide Tambo.

PREVIOUS PAGES, RIGHT: The way they were as young lawyer activists and in December 1990 when, after more than three decades in exile, Oliver Tambo was welcomed home by his old comrade.

OPPOSITE LEFT: The early years after his release brought for Mandela a succession of reunions and, sadly, a number of final farewells. In January, 1995, stalwart of the liberation movement Joe Slovo died. Standing in front of this immense blow-up of the South African Communist Party national chairman and former *Umkhonto weSizwe* chief of staff, President Mandela remembered Slovo as 'one of the greatest South African and African revolutionaries of our times'.

ABOVE: Oliver Tambo and Nelson Mandela pay their last respects to another friend and anti-apartheid activist at the funeral in January 1993 of Helen Joseph, champion of human rights and, said Mandela, a woman who helped to shape South Africa's destiny.

LEFT: HENNER FRANKENFELD/PICTURENET AFRICA

Comrades

COURTESY: HELMUT SCHNEIDER/PHOTOGRAPHER: TREVOR SACHS.

Helmut and Veda Schneider had been living at their Rivonia home *Lilliesleaf* with their children Kirstin and Sebastian for about a year when one summer day in 1991, they had an unexpected visitor. It was the man soon to become South Africa's president, Nelson Mandela. Recalls Veda: 'The whole household was thrown into a panic, but he immediately put us at ease and asked if he could please wander around.' They followed him around the house and garden with mounting excitement as he pointed out places he remembered — 'this is where we hid our papers, that is where I slept, this is the tree where a little boy made me feel ashamed for shooting a bird, over there is where we buried a caché of weapons' — and shared his sentimental journey. Mandela's visit confirmed the stories they had heard about their house; this was where, posing as gardener 'David Motsamayi', Mandela used it as one of his hide-outs while operating underground after the ANC was banned in 1960. It was here, too, while he was in jail, that members of the High Command of *Umkhonto weSizwe* were arrested during a police raid. The result was life imprisonment on Robben Island for most of them. Subsequently the Schneiders organised a lunch at *Lilliesleaf* in February, 1994, for Mandela and some of the men arrested there in July, 1963. Veda remembers that the reunion lunch, far from being the serious affair she expected, was lighthearted and salted with humour as the former conspirators laughed about past amateurish activities and disguises. Mandela was charming and radiated an immediate sense of spontaneous warmth. 'The same afternoon a beautiful flower arrangement with a personal note from Mr Mandela arrived. I thought that gesture of thanks was very special,' she says.

ABOVE: Pictured in the garden at the Rivonia reunion are (from left) Ahmed Kathrada, Lionel Bernstein, Helmut and Veda Schneider, Nelson Mandela, Kirstin Schneider, Andrew Mlangeni and Walter Sisulu.

Madiba

Comrades

Amina Cachalia has been a friend of Nelson Mandela and a supporter of the liberation struggle since meeting him in the late 1940s, when she was involved in the work of the youth wing of the South African Indian Congress, of which her late husband, Yusuf, was secretary.

Early in 1961, while Mandela was still operating underground, there was a knock one morning at the door of her home in Pageview, Johannesburg. 'When I opened it I found a man dressed as a night watchman, wearing a cap and dangling earrings. It was a good disguise, but I recognised Nelson from his boxer's physique. Another time he lived with us for 12 days at the home of friends in Jeppe, where we stayed to avoid being arrested and detained during ANC strike action. I got to know him very well, as we used to play cards and Ludo night and day and have political discussions. He loves gardening and while there he dug up a little patch of their backyard and made them a flower garden. He has never forgotten them, he has a memory like an elephant. He is very caring and loyal and never forgets friends or people that stood by him or supported the struggle.'

Mrs Cachalia has cooked many a meal for Mandela and while he is fond of a good curry he confessed to her that often when faced with a state banquet on his travels overseas he yearned for the *umphothulo* (maize porridge and sour milk) and *umngqusho* (samp and beans) of his boyhood years in Transkei.

TOP: Surrounded by old friends and prominent struggle activists, Nelson Mandela prepares to do justice to one of his favourite curries at a 75th birthday lunch cooked up by Amina Cachalia at her Johannesburg home. From left are Mrs Cachalia, Ethel Walt of the Black Sash and Rica Hodgson.

CENTRE: Nelson Mandela takes time out to prepare a speech for the ANC Youth League.

RIGHT: Amina Cachalia is an attentive audience as he practises the speech.

Madiba

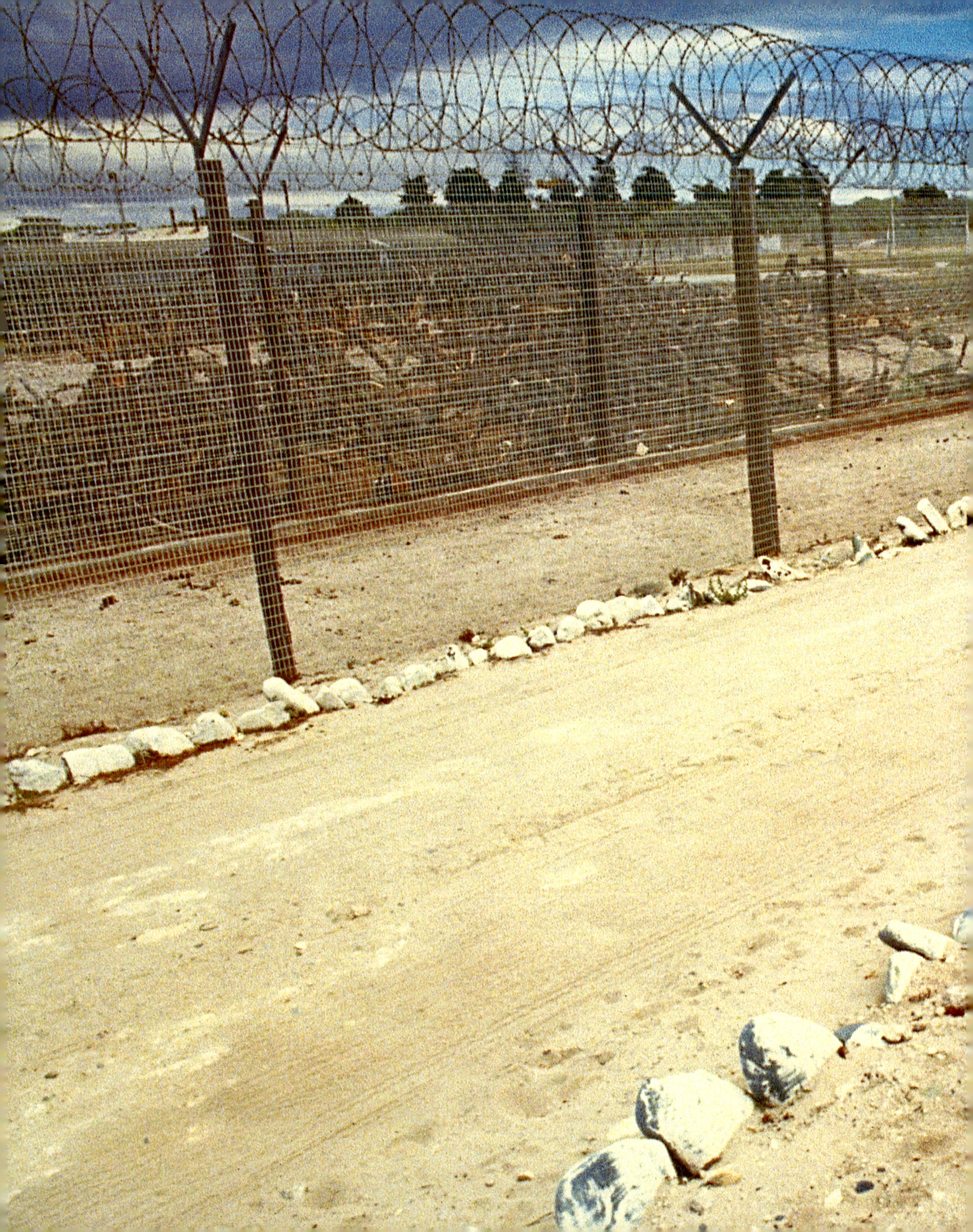

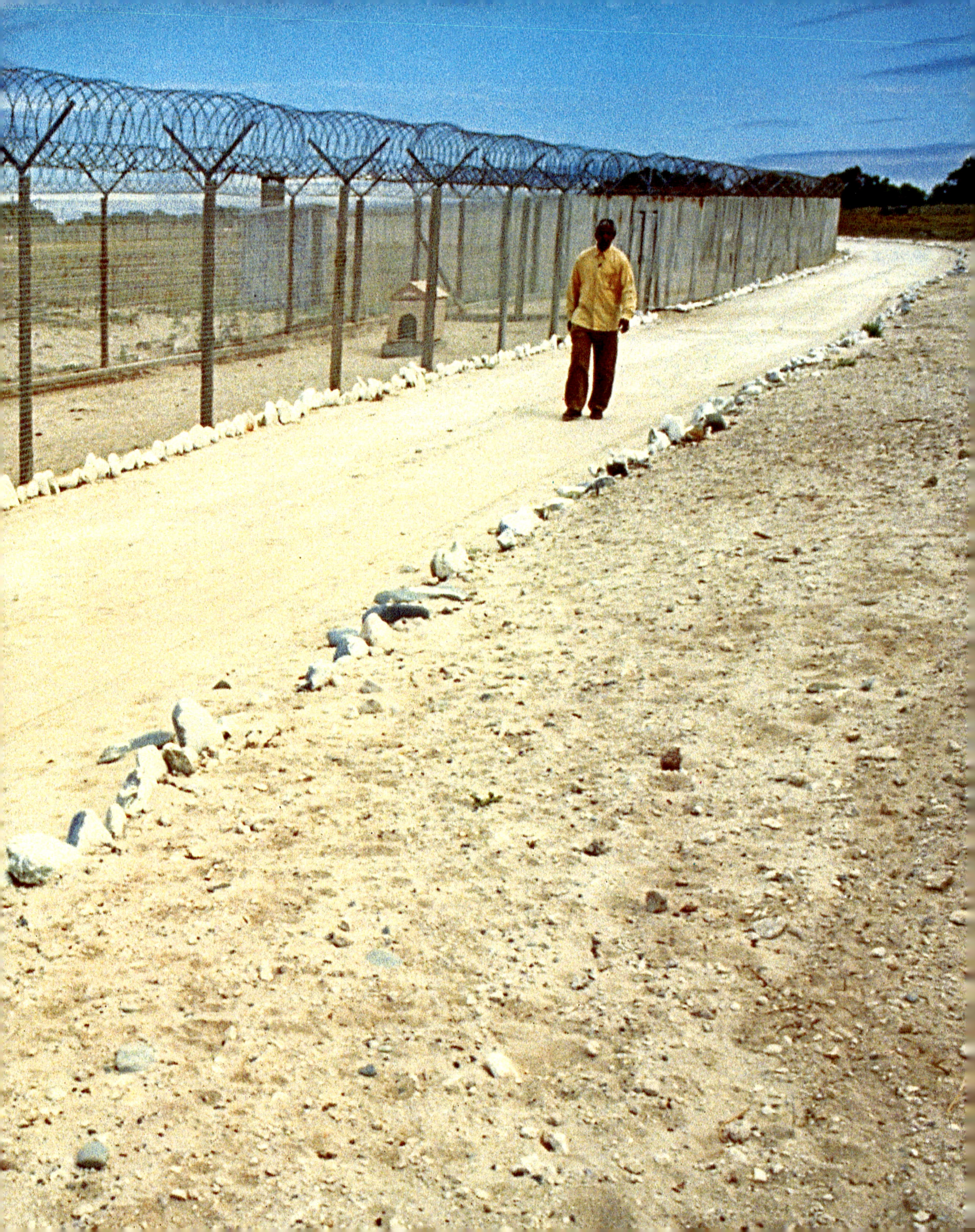

↣ Victors

RETURN TO THE ISLAND

A summer wind flicked gustily at the Atlantic swells rolling into Table Bay on February 11, 1994, as the broad, blue–hulled Robben Island ferry *Proteus* churned its way through Cape Town's Victoria Basin towards the breakwater, then swung northward. Ahead, visible in glimpses over the unsteady deck, lay the dark hump of South Africa's notorious prison island.

It is a sombre nine–kilometre journey, even on the brightest of days, like this one; a 45–minute trip that is invested with a forlorn sense of apartheid's wasteful decades. This February Friday, though, was different. It was four years to the day after Nelson Mandela's release. He was returning to Robben Island with five fellow Rivonia trialists for a reunion that would seem to expunge from apartheid's Alcatraz all the fearsome potency it once had.

Five elderly men, smiling and talkative, were on the boat, each in a knot of journalists. Walter Sisulu, Govan Mbeki, Ahmed Kathrada, Denis Goldberg and Andrew Mlangeni were having their memories stirred. It was quite a chatty business; they hadn't forgotten a thing, though it was plain they had forgiven much.

President Mandela was spared the swells. He was flown to the island by helicopter but was at the quay, an uncanny figure of authority among respectful prison officials, when the *Proteus* berthed. Thirty years before, when they'd flown to the island in 1964, to begin their life sentences, it was not like this at all. Watching the ex–prisoners disembarking in 1994, and greeting the jailers — though not the same ones

PREVIOUS PAGES: For years Nelson Mandela saw this fence from the other side. Here he walks on the outside of the prison perimeter at Robben Island on his return visit in February 1994. Here was apartheid at its starkest — no black warders, no white prisoners.
PHOTOGRAPH: ©KARINA TUROK AND ISLAND PICTURES.

RIGHT: Four years after his release from a mainland jail Nelson Mandela revisits the cramped cell in B Section that was his home for 18 long years on the prison island, nine kilometres out in the icy Atlantic from Cape Town. He describes Robben Island as 'without question the harshest, most iron–fisted outpost in the South African penal system'.

PHOTOGRAPH BY JÜRGEN SCHADEBERG

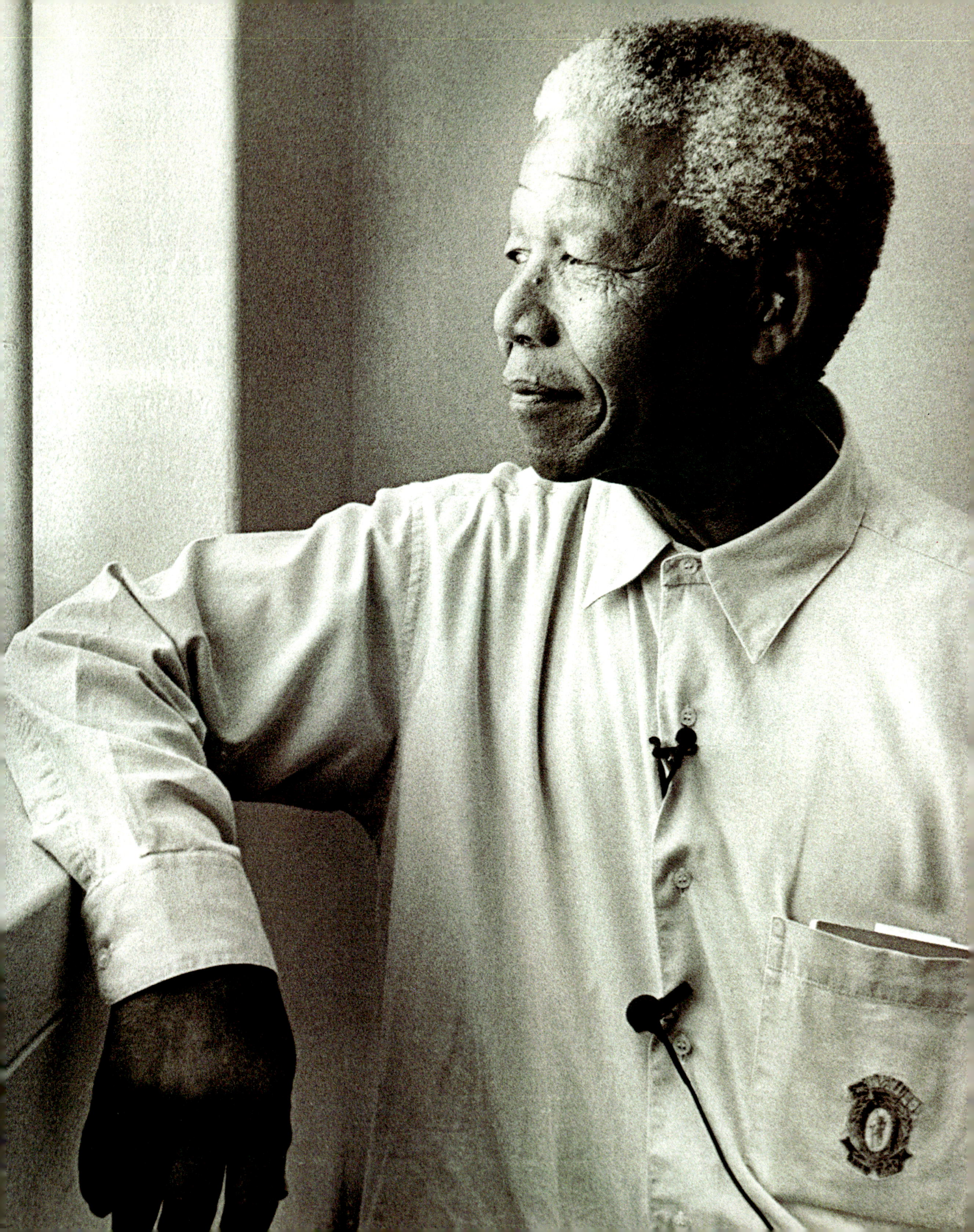

⇥ Victors

— with uncomplicated ease it was hard to imagine a more complete about–turn.

The cold, grey slate facility that was once abuzz with the polemics of revolt, that rattled with sharp commands, or murmured with the commonplace chit–chat of wistful men behind bars, seemed transformed. Now, in 1994, there was laughter and reminiscence, but there was nothing flippant about it. President Mandela had been back at least once before, in 1993 — but it must still have been deeply affecting, returning to his barred cell, tramping across the lime quarry, hearing the incessant tease of the unseen sea...

In the dining–room of the restored colonial residence, once the island governor's home, the gathering of fêted ex–lifers, journalists and prison officials, lunched on roast chicken and vegetables, washed down with a specially bottled 'Robben Island Pinotage' organised by his eager island hosts.

President Mandela spoke for almost an hour. It was an expansive, informal address. He wished, on the advice of those close to him, to 'personalise the collective experience of prison', something he said he found difficult. He spoke of the shattering experiences of those years, the awful conditions, the psychological persecution, the isolation. Pain clouded his face when he recalled how, not long after a visit from his mother in 1968, he received news that she had died, but was refused permission to attend her funeral.

Barely a year later he learned by telegram

RIGHT: Nelson Mandela relives old times with other Rivonia trialists in the island lime quarry where they toiled daily for nearly 13 years in work that left him with serious eye problems. They turned the time to good account by using the quarry as a 'university' where study groups were formed and Walter Sisulu gave political history lectures to a younger generation of prisoners.

LOUISE GUBB/i-AFRIKA

Victors

of the death of his oldest son, Thembi, in a car accident.

This, and the heartless indifference of the authorities, had left him devastated, he recalled. 'Of course,' he mused, 'the wounds that cannot be seen are more painful than those that can be treated by a doctor. I did not share my pain with anyone.'

He returned over and over again to the inspiring features of island life; the unshakeable fraternal bonds and the seriousness with which he and his fellow prisoners had shouldered the responsibility of remaining true to their convictions, and of debating them responsibly, even under conditions which must have cast doubt on their ever being able to share them, freely, with the country.

He chose this speech to reveal how he had acted alone, after 'agonising' soul-searching, in initiating talks in the mid-1980s with the government of then President PW Botha, the first step towards negotiations.

In November, 1984, while incarcerated at Pollsmoor Prison on the mainland, Nelson Mandela believed the time ripe to bridge the chasm between the banned African National Congress and the National Party government — but he did not consult, or even tell, his fellow leaders or prison comrades. It was indeed an agonising dilemma.

'I felt I had a duty to see them before approaching the authorities, but I knew that if I did, they would reject it,' he said.

He went ahead and arranged a meeting with then Justice Minister Kobie Coetsee.

LEFT: Nelson Mandela in the Robben Island lime quarry where he worked with pick and shovel in much the same way that exiles and dissidents toiled from the time governor Jan van Riebeeck banished the first political prisoner — 'Harry the Strandloper' — to the island in 1658.

Madiba

⇥ Victors

During his time on Robben Island, Nelson Mandela developed serious eye problems. RIGHT: President Mandela with Dr Percy Amoils, the Johannesburg ophthalmic surgeon who operated on his eye in July, 1994. Another distinguished patient of Dr Amoils was Margaret Thatcher, whose sight was saved by his system of cryosurgery. This gained him the Queen's Award in 1975.

COURTESY: DR PERCY AMOILS

When he felt the debate was 'concrete', he asked to see his four colleagues — Walter Sisulu, Ahmed Kathrada, Andrew Mlangeni and Raymond Mhlaba — calculating that 'if I convinced Walter Sisulu, he would help to convince the rest.' They talked it over.

'He was very diplomatic. He said he was not against it but would have preferred the government to start first. I replied: "If you are not against negotiations, then it doesn't matter. I have started."'

The next step was to inform the exiled leadership. 'I smuggled out a letter and a reply came back from Oliver Tambo. There was a note of disapproval. He said: "What are you discussing?" I replied in one line: "I am discussing a meeting between the ANC and the government. Full stop."'

Eventually, leaders of the ANC, the Youth League, the Women's League and the Congress of South African Trade Unions were informed. 'Not a single person said no,' recalled President Mandela. The meeting with Coetsee was followed by talks with PW Botha, which Mandela remembered as 'one of the best meetings I have ever had'.

President Mandela praised Kobie Coetsee as 'the man who not only opened the way for a meeting with then President FW de Klerk, but risked his political career at a time when no single member of the National Party was prepared to be associated with us. He had courage and vision'.

President Mandela also remembered that it was not always sober political exchanges that exercised his and the other prisoners' minds. A long debate, whose whimsy more than compensated for its lack of *gravitas*, was the question of whether or not there were tigers in Africa.

The island was more than a jail to the redoubtable figures who posed patiently at their former cells on their 1994 visit, who crossed and re–crossed the lime quarry so that every photographer might get a good picture.

Their return, as quiet, self–assured victors, not visibly embittered, was the remarkable proof of it. — MICHAEL MORRIS, SPECIAL WRITER, CAPE ARGUS.

Victors

In the spring of 1996, President Mandela revisited the last jail to hold him, Victor Verster Prison, near Paarl, from whose gates he walked to freedom and enduring fame in February, 1990.

ABOVE LEFT: Nelson Mandela with his former warder and chef, Warrant Officer Jack Swart, at his former jail home at Victor Verster Prison.

ABOVE RIGHT: Nelson Mandela embraces one of his former prison warders in a touching display of forgiveness and reconciliation.

LEFT: Ever the fatherly figure, President Mandela kisses the hand of another inmate, the daughter of a prison warder. The Freedom of Paarl was conferred on him during this visit.

Madiba

✢ Transition

LOUISE GUBB/i-AFRIKA

THE DAWN OF DEMOCRACY

Nelson Mandela was not only a prime behind–the–scenes player in negotiations that began the transitional process to democracy which astounded South Africans as much as it did observers in other countries; he was also the initiator of the talks and the person who, away from the prying eyes of press and public, drove the whole political exchange. As much as anything, the negotiations were a tribute to his acumen and foresight, sharpened in the solitude of a prison cell over the years.

✢ 58   *Madiba*

Transition

In 1983, when President PW Botha ushered in the tricameral parliamentary system — which catered for all race groups except blacks — he offered the imprisoned ANC leader his freedom, provided he left the country or agreed to settle in the then nominally independent Transkei homeland. Mandela rejected the offer outright. He once again reiterated his views, first expressed long before the ANC even took up arms in 1960, to fight apartheid, that a national convention or all–party congress had to take place to allow all South Africans, through their elected representatives, to discuss the future of the country.

M*andela never gave up* on this idea. Even as the National Party regime dug in its heels at the height of its repression in the mid–1980s and consequent punitive economic sanctions from some sections of the international community began to bite harshly, Nelson Mandela continued to petition for dialogue. Without a mandate from his colleagues in prison on Robben Island or those in exile in Zambia, he wrote from Victor Verster Prison to PW Botha suggesting a one–on–one parley.

This was an extremely risky and dangerous suggestion for Mandela to make, both for himself and Botha. If anything regarding his proposal leaked out, young activists inside the country and in exile could question his sanity and say he was eventually breaking in prison or getting soft in his old age. Yet he persisted, knowing what the risks were. First he held a series of preparatory meetings with Kobie Coetsee, the Minister of Justice, and ended up taking tea at Tuynhuys in Cape Town with his jailer, Botha.

That, then, is the origin of the multi–party talks which finally culminated in the adoption, at the World Trade Centre near Johannesburg on November 17, 1993, of South Africa's Interim Constitution, in terms of which the country's founding democratic general elections were held just over five months later.

LOUISE GUBB/i-AFRIKA

After Botha stepped down in August, 1989, Mandela continued to engage Coetsee and Botha's successor, FW de Klerk, in dialogue. This process gained momentum after Mandela's release from prison and he flew to Lusaka to brief his colleagues on the talks he had been having with the government. In May, 1990, Mandela led a top–level ANC delegation to Cape Town for historic talks with the government. Agreements reached came to be known as the Groote Schuur Minute. This was shortly followed by the Pretoria Minute, in terms of which an accord relating to the return of exiles was reached.

From then on official negotiations were in full swing and were joined by other political parties and organisations. From December 19 to 21, 1990, they all met at the World Trade Centre in what came to be known as the Convention for a Democratic South Africa (Codesa), to lay the foundations for the transition to democracy. The talks went well until De Klerk stood up to blame the ANC for the violence which was sweeping through some parts of the country at the time.

Mandela, who had already spoken, insisted on being allowed to respond. He made a blistering personal attack on the man who, on the day of his release from prison, he hailed as 'a man of integrity'. The talks ended on a sour note but, as was later to be characteristic of them, the process was rescued by one–on–one discussions between the two principals, Mandela and De Klerk, who agreed to sink their differences.

Violence, over which the two leaders traded verbal blows, had reached frightening proportions in the country at the time. Although it had been largely confined to KwaZulu–Natal from the days of conflict between the Inkatha Freedom Party and the United Democratic Front/Mass Democratic

OPPOSITE: Cape Town, May, 1990, and Nelson Mandela and FW de Klerk, backed by their negotiating teams, hold a press conference after their first round of talks on transition.

ABOVE: Nelson Mandela has good reason to be in high spirits. He is attending, in Durban, the first African National Congress conference on South African soil in 30 years.

Madiba 59

Transition

Movement axis in the mid–1980s, after the signing of the Pretoria Minute political violence spilled over with a vengeance into Gauteng (then known as the Pretoria–Witwatersrand–Vereeniging area). Late in April a group of hostel dwellers in the black townships of Boipatong and Sebokeng had attacked and killed some township residents aligned to the ANC and, in protest, the organisation postponed by a fortnight, its scheduled talks with the government in Groote Schuur, Cape Town. From there the violence spread to Soweto and various East Rand townships, such as Katlehong, Thokoza, Vosloorus, and KwaThema. Involved in the conflict were, largely, members of the IFP and ANC, although many people aligned to neither political organisation were caught in the crossfire.

Mandela and his colleagues in the ANC had a strong suspicion that the violence was being deliberately orchestrated by forces opposed to peace and bent on postponing — or making impossible — the holding of free and fair elections. For this reason, the organisation repeatedly urged that haste was of the utmost importance in the talks. To move the talks forward at the pace it wanted, the organisation also found itself having to make a series of compromises, such as on the existence and powers of provincial governments, on the number of votes to be cast in the April 27, 1994, elections and on power–sharing in the proposed Government of National Unity. Although, like other political principals, he was not to be found at the World Trade Centre where the Negotiating Council and various sub–committees met and did the actual bargaining, Mandela always loomed large in the background. Such ANC negotiators as Cyril Ramaphosa, Mohammed Valli Moosa and Mac Maharaj kept him informed at all times, and he gave instructions and generally directed the process from the wings.

LOUISE GUBB/i-AFRIKA

To resolve deadlocks, Mandela would phone De Klerk or IFP leader Chief Mangosuthu Buthelezi to discuss issues with them and, in De Klerk's case, meet him personally. While Mandela did not feature in the democracy talks as prominently as, say, the ANC's Cyril Ramaphosa or the NP's chief negotiator, Roelf Meyer, he was central to them. So concerned was he about stability in the transitional period that, even before he became president, he held secret talks with then South African Police Commissioner General Johann van der Merwe and South African Defence Force Chief General Georg Meiring to ensure they would support a democratically elected government.

LOUISE GUBB/i-AFRIKA

It was very much in character, then, that on the day of his inauguration as president of the Republic of South Africa, Mandela struck a conciliatory note and made reconciliation across the racial divide the main plank of his government's policies. He publicly embraced De Klerk during an impromptu address to the crowds gathered in front of the Union Buildings and lifted De Klerk's and Thabo Mbeki's hands above his head, much to the delight of the multiracial crowd. — *Kaizer M Nyatsumba, deputy editor, The Mercury.*

Transition

OPPOSITE TOP: Violence sweeps the country as the negotiating process picks up pace. Here, Nelson Mandela pays his respects to mourners after a massacre during an ANC night vigil in Sebokeng, near Johannesburg.

OPPOSITE BELOW: Nothing doing... Reluctant to participate in negotiations until his conditions are met, Chief Mangosuthu Buthelezi, head of the Inkatha Freedom Party, appears to decline to shake hands with Nelson Mandela and FW de Klerk.

ABOVE: Smiles all round as FW de Klerk and Nelson Mandela lead their chief negotiators, the ANC's Cyril Ramaphosa and the National Party's Roelf Meyer, from another round of talks.

Madiba   61

MANDELA FOR PRESIDENT
THE PEOPLE'S CHOICE!
MANDELA FOR PRESIDENT
ANC

Elections

FREEDOM AT LAST

There was a tangible air of excitement throughout South Africa at the end of April, 1994, as millions of people of all races happily mingled in seemingly never–ending serpentine queues to put the final public seal on the country's miraculous march to democracy. This was the first time in South Africa's history that all its peoples had gone to the polls together to elect a truly representative government, and the fact that most of the voters had to wait for anything up to 12 hours in broiling sun did nothing to diminish the festive air that some hard political bargaining and nearly nine decades of waiting had caused to sweep through the land — the last breath of the mighty wind of change that only began to blow through the continent at the end of World War II.

LOUISE GUBB/i-AFRIKA

OPPOSITE: Cheering supporters surround Nelson Mandela at an ANC rally at Mmabatho, held to celebrate the ousting of the Bophuthatswana homeland president, Lucas Mangope, shortly before the 1994 elections. Mangope's overthrow paved the way for the homeland's reincorporation into South Africa.

ABOVE: Not even a presidential candidate and national icon is immune from the lighter side of the hustings.

LEFT: LOUISE GUBB/i-AFRIKA

Madiba

↯ Elections

GEORGE HALLETT

↯ 64   *Madiba*

Elections

OPPOSITE: Nelson Mandela prepares for his upcoming TV confrontation with President FW de Klerk with the help of Johannesburg journalist Allister Sparks (left) who played the part of the National Party leader in a mock debate.

LEFT: 'Now is the Time' proclaims an elaborate poster as Nelson Mandela continues on his long election campaign trail.

SALLY SHORKEND/PICTURENET AFRICA

PAUL VELASCO/PICTURENET AFRICA

ABOVE: ... and the real thing. Mandela and De Klerk square up in a televised debate watched by an estimated five million people.

GEORGE HALLETT

Madiba 65

⁂ Elections

RIGHT: On April 27, 1994, at the age of 76, Nelson Mandela casts the first vote of his life in the country of his birth. He voted at Ohlange High School, Inanda, north of Durban, close to the spot where John Dube, the ANC's first president, lies buried. After casting his vote Mandela said the occasion was the realisation of hopes and dreams cherished for decades — dreams of a South Africa representing all South Africans as one nation.

WALTER DHLADLA

⁂ 66 *Madiba*

Elections

ABOVE: A congratulatory hug for Nelson Mandela from Dimpho Hani, widow of slain South African Communist Party leader Chris Hani, at celebrations to mark the ANC's sweeping victory in the country's first democratic elections. ANC secretary–general Cyril Ramaphosa looks on.

LEFT: The culmination of the negotiation and election process... ANC negotiator Cyril Ramaphosa triumphantly holds aloft a copy of South Africa's new constitution signed by President Mandela

Madiba

Inauguration

ABOVE: An historic moment as Nelson Mandela is sworn in as the country's first democratically elected President at his inauguration at Union Buildings, Pretoria, on May 10, 1994.

RIGHT: Outgoing President FW de Klerk looks on as Nelson Mandela signs for the first time as President of the Republic of South Africa.

PAUL VELASCO/ABPL

Madiba

Inauguration

LOUISE GUBB/I-AFRIKA

LEFT: The flag that has flown over South Africa since Union exactly 84 years ago is hauled down for the last time at the inauguration ceremony.

Madiba

Integration

ABOVE: All together now... President Mandela flanked by (from left) Deputy President Thabo Mbeki, Frene Ginwala, Speaker of the House, former Minister of Justice Kobie Coetsee and Deputy President FW de Klerk.

BELOW LEFT: Mandela thanks the police at Ezakheni, Natal, for their assistance during the elections, and (right) confers with South African Defence Force Chief, Gen Georg Meiring during a military parade in Pietersburg.

Integration

Nothing set the seal more on the transition to a new South Africa after President Mandela's inauguration than the integration into the South African National Defence Force of 15 000 members of the ANC's military wing, *Umkhonto weSizwe* (Spear of the Nation), and the Azanian People's Liberation Army (Apla). Pictures at left show the SANDF's new Commander–in–Chief's hands–on approach to what became a tricky tansformation.

BELOW: Always ready to extend the hand of friendship.

Madiba 71

RODGER BOSCH/ABPL

RODGER BOSCH/i-AFRICA

During his inauguration as the first democratically elected President of South Africa, Nelson Mandela described FW de Klerk as one of Africa's greatest sons. And the world agreed. A shared Nobel Peace Prize confirmed the inaugural view that these two men from worlds apart had wrought a miracle by steering South Africa from the brink of outright civil war.

De Klerk was the privileged Afrikaner, the last President of the apartheid era, the man who announced on February 2, 1990, the momentous decision to release Nelson Mandela from prison. Nelson Mandela was a scion of the Xhosa Royal House who had been jailed for 27 years by a regime which had ruthlessly crushed two generations of resistance to racial segregation.

Would the one do what few others had done in history and agree to share and to eventually give up power and privilege? And if so, would the other take up that power and privilege without retribution? The miracle lay not only in the fact that they negotiated a settlement, but that they remained steadfast in the face of provocative and often violent acts perpetrated by forces determined to derail their delicate negotiations to set South Africa on the road to democracy.

WORLDS APART

The inaugural view of their relationship was only an occasional one. They often clashed, sometimes publicly, but it is understandable for two people not to get on well with each other when the one faces the consequences of his decision to become simply a player and the other pursues his right to challenge for paramountcy.

Even in the triumphant days before they accepted the Nobel Peace Prize late in 1993, they had grown steadily apart. FW de Klerk stood motionless behind Nelson Mandela as he was sworn in as President of South Africa at the Union Buildings in Pretoria on May 10, 1994. Barely two years later, on June 30, 1996, FW de Klerk finally resigned from the Government of National Unity led by President Mandela.

He had hoped his early departure would give him the opportunity to build his National Party into a multi–racial opposition alliance which could challenge President Mandela's African National Congress in national elections scheduled for 1999. By early 1997, his National Party was faltering as some of its most senior members resigned in disillusionment and set out to form their own opposition alliance.

⁂ Crossroads

ABOVE: President Mandela and FW de Klerk at a mass at Gosforth Park race–track, Germiston, given by Pope John Paul II during his visit to South Africa in September, 1995.

RIGHT: A grim–faced Mandela after meeting President FW de Klerk in Pretoria to discuss the countrywide violence threatening to derail negotiations leading up to democratic elections.

Crossroads

ABOVE: Reflecting the feelings of many South Africans, Archbishop Desmond Tutu expresses his delight by applauding the televised presentation to Nelson Mandela and then President FW de Klerk of the joint 1993 Nobel Peace Prize in Oslo, which they shared in recognition of their labours to usher South Africa into a democratic new era. Archbishop Tutu was awarded the Nobel Peace Prize in 1984.

LEFT: New laureate Mandela proudly displays his Nobel Peace Prize medallion. In his acceptance speech in Oslo he said the triumph of democracy in South Africa brought to a close 500 years of African colonisation that began with the establishment of the Portuguese empire.

Madiba

ORANJE ONTWIKKELING
in die
HARTLAND
van die
AFRIKANER

'N NALATENSKAP VAN

HENDRIK FRENCH
VERWOERD
8 SEPTEMBER 1901 – 6 SEPTEMBER 1966
ONTHUL DEUR MEV. BETSIE VERWOERD
ORANIA, 22 MEI 1993

Reconciliation

BURYING THE PAST

In 1995 Nelson Mandela and a small entourage paid a visit to Betsie Verwoerd, the 94 year–old widow of Hendrik French Verwoerd, chief theorist and principal architect of the policy of apartheid, and Prime Minister of the Republic of South Africa until he was assassinated in 1966. Mrs Verwoerd lives in Orania, a village of 500 souls in the Northern Cape Province, established as an Afrikaner refuge on the banks of the Orange River in 1991. This visit, more than anything, symbolises President Mandela's deep commitment to national reconciliation and is tellingly recalled by his long–time friend and fellow activist, *Amina Cachalia*, who accompanied him.

❛The visit to Orania was President Mandela's idea. He told me he wanted to get the wives of the old guard, the people that were in power before, and some of us older generation of women together. He said we must talk to these people and reconcile. I asked him what we should talk to these women about? We didn't know them, they didn't know us and we were always virtually enemies. What were we going to say to them? He said, "Come on, you know what to say to them. Talk to them, it's a good thing to learn how they feel. Make them feel comfortable in the new set–up."

We had invited Betsie Verwoerd to a function in Pretoria but her doctors said that she shouldn't undertake the journey, so she said when Mr Mandela was in the area she would love to entertain him to a cup of coffee. He

LEFT: The man who started it and the man who ended it. President Mandela stands in silence at the memorial in Orania, Northern Cape, to Hendrik French Verwoerd, Prime Minister of South Africa and chief architect of the National Party's policy of apartheid.

WALTER DHLADLA

Madiba

ⵣ Reconciliation

decided that he would go and see her. Albertina Sisulu and I went with him by helicopter to Orania. It's a dreadful place, stark, dusty. It was the end of winter when we went and everything was grey, with not a blade of grass nor hardly a tree to be seen.

It reminded me of the beginnings of the days of the Group Areas Act when we went to look at Lenasia, the area for Asians, one day when it first started and there were just a few council houses dotted all over this dusty, miserable place.

Orania looked very much like that. There were these funny little homes and none of the people looked happy. Mrs Verwoerd is old now and she is frail but she is very much alert still. I spoke to her in Afrikaans and she was very thrilled.

WALTER DHLADLA

ABOVE: Under the gaze of famous Boer General Koos de la Rey, 'The Lion of the Western Transvaal', President Mandela pays a visit to the Historical Rifle Museum in Orania.

RIGHT: President Mandela signs the visitors' book on his arrival at the Afrikaner settlement of Orania.

WALTER DHLADLA

78 Madiba

Reconciliation

LEFT: Nonagenarian Mrs Betsie Verwoerd, widow of Dr Hendrik Verwoerd, listens intently to Mandela's speech before sharing in the general laughter at one of the President's sallies.

Madiba 79

Reconciliation

They were polite to us, but here was a group of people that I don't think one can reconcile with, or rather that they would not like to reconcile with others because they want to continue separate development. They want to be on their own with their own people. We chatted to her and had *koeksusters, melktert* and *soetkoek* and all the lovely things that the Afrikaners make. Mrs Verwoerd met the President, they shook hands and she read out her speech from a letter. It said she was very happy to have met him, she wished him well, and said she was very happy living in Orania. President Mandela answered that he was happy to be there and said that while the past would always be there we had to go on. He hoped that they would go along with us. Then we all walked to Verwoerd's memorial. We stood there for a while, and I said to myself, "Amina, did you ever think you'd be standing at the memorial of the man who caused so much pain to so many people, including yourself?"

Back in the helicopter the President asked me what I thought of the visit and I told him I thought these people would never reconcile with us, that they wanted to live on their own with people who spoke their language and were from their own culture. I asked him how he expected ever to get people like this to realise that they were living in the new South Africa.

He replied, "They will, they'll come right in the end."

ABOVE AND RIGHT: Mrs Verwoerd reads from her specially prepared speech and welcomes President Mandela to Orania.

WALTER DHLADLA

HENNER FRANKENFELD/PICTURENET AFRICA

Madiba

Reconciliation

LEFT: Mrs Verwoerd enjoys a tête–a–tête with her famous visitor, during which he tells her about his plans for the country. Afterwards she said she had been impressed by his unshakeable calmness – and his height.

BELOW: A resident of Orania bids farewell as President Mandela's helicopter lifts off.

COURTESY: AMINA CACHALIA
WALTER DHLADLA

☘ Reconciliation

WALTER DHLADLA

WALTER DHLADLA

☘ 82   *Madiba*

Reconciliation

WALTER DHLADLA

WALTER DHLADLA

The famous admonitory finger of former State President PW Botha is very much in evidence at this meeting between Nelson Mandela and the man feared by his political enemies as *Die Groot Krokodil* – 'the Great Crocodile' – although he finally succumbs to the equally famous Mandela charm. Despite Botha's reputation, Mandela describes him as 'unfailingly courteous, deferential and friendly'.

Madiba

Reconciliation

WALTER DHLADLA

LOUISE GUBB/i-AFRIKA

84 *Madiba*

Reconciliation

OPPOSITE, TOP: Elize Botha, wife of former State President PW Botha, chats to President Mandela at a reconciliation lunch in 1995, for wives and widows of former Heads of State and veterans of the anti-apartheid struggle organised by Amina Cachalia (centre) at his official Pretoria residence, *Mahlamba'ndlopfu* — Tsonga for 'Dawn of the Day'. Seated is Mrs Emily Orpa Nokwe, mother of the late Duma Nokwe, one-time secretary-general of the ANC and the first black advocate in the Transvaal.

OPPOSITE BOTTOM: President Mandela's spirit of reconciliation extends even to the man who played a part in putting him behind bars for 27 years. Dr Percy Yutar was Deputy Attorney-General of the Transvaal and State prosecutor when Nelson Mandela and other members of the ANC and the South African Communist Party were sentenced to life imprisonment in June, 1964, on charges of sabotage and conspiring to overthrow the government. Here, at the President's official Pretoria residence, he recalls the past with the man he sent to Robben Island.

LEFT: Elize Botha strolls with President Mandela in front of the house that, as Libertas, was once her home. Mrs Botha passed away in mid-1997.

WALTER DHLADLA

Madiba

LOUISE GUBB/i-AFRIKA

Nelson Mandela is unique in many respects, not least in that he is probably the only head of state in the world to have pledged one–third of his annual salary as President of South Africa for five years to establish and sustain a children's fund dedicated to the upliftment and care of the nation's disadvantaged youngsters.

Since he announced the foundation of the Nelson Mandela Children's Fund (NMCF) in May, 1995, emphasising the priority he gives to the welfare of children in the new South Africa, the fund has become monumental in its scope.

In its efforts to alleviate the plight of disadvantaged youth it has, with its alliance partners, reached into far corners of often traumatised communities to spread cheer and bring hope for a better future. Its work has drawn support from all walks of life, all levels of society and from countries throughout the world inspired by the President's noble crusade for a more caring approach to the nation's youth.

Such support ranges from the likes of United States of America and international businessman Teddy Forstmann, the NMCF's biggest and most consistent benefactor at more than US$1.75 million to date, to a former street child who donates R150 of his salary every quarter in appreciation of help which gave him the opportunity to become an earning and contributing member of society.

Donations and pledges have poured more than R50 million into the NMCF in just over two years of operations, and the Fund has disbursed more than R12 million in 634 projects initiated by 355 separate non–government organisations, touching and improving the lives of hundreds of thousands of young people.

Major beneficiaries include institutions caring for homeless, abused, abandoned, and disabled children, as well as those providing education, places to play in safety, and disaster relief, and others involved in the rehabilitation of young offenders.

86 *Madiba*

Children

As President Mandela points out: 'We come from a past in which the lives of our children were assaulted and devastated in many ways, particularly by the destruction of the vital chain of institutions essential to the healthy transformation of children into well functioning adults — the family home, the neighbourhood communal structures, an effective educational environment and the wider socio–economic support system. High levels of violence, homelessness, poor nutrition, lack of facilities in the form of health services, clean water, sanitation and places to play in safety have helped to shatter many of our young people's physical, emotional and spiritual resources so essential to human dignity. One of our highest priorities must therefore be our children – for our children are our nation's future.'

The magnitude of the task facing the Fund is starkly underscored by the fact that 37 per cent of South Africa's population is under the age of 15, and a further 11 million or 24 per cent are in the 16–30 age bracket, of which 52 per cent are unemployed.

By the year 2000 more than half of the population will be under 21 – a factor that will throw the necessity for President Mandela's brainchild into even sharper relief.

The Fund is dedicated to inspiring such efforts and to acting as a catalyst for institutions, organisations, corporate business and individuals who realise the importance to the country of helping the young to realise their potential and promise.

The NMCF sees among those at risk young people who are growing to adulthood in a socio–economic environment of deep deprivation which would, in the ordinary course of their development, deny them access to:

- Adequate nutrition, and living conditions which provide adequate shelter, free from gross overcrowding and with reasonable access to potable water, basic health care delivery services and places to play in safety;

- The means to be protected from physical, emotional and sexual abuse and to have access to remediation where lack of such protection results in damage; and

- Adequate schooling, particularly at the pre–primary and primary levels, to provide them with the basic tools which will enable them to develop their individual potential.

Also at risk are disabled young people – especially those with no access to existing products and services providing a protected and physically tolerable standard of life; and those facing habitual delinquency who need and desire an appropriate rehabilitative environment, strongly aligned to a work and learning ethic.

To achieve these aims the NMCF networks with all role players in the field, and while it does initiate and develop projects and provide shelter, provisions, clothing, physical aids, training and equipment, it always works in close alliance with grantees — existing and new non–government and community–based organisations.

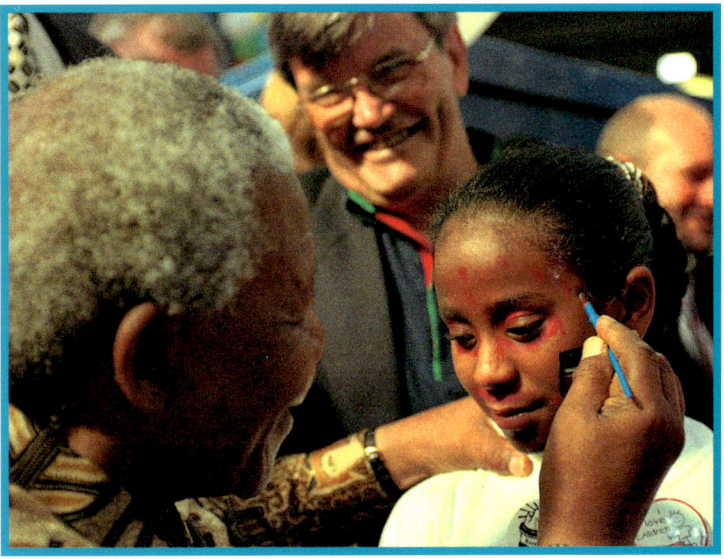

LOUISE GUBB/i-AFRIKA

Says President Mandela: 'There can be no keener revelation of a society's soul than the way in which it treats its children' and notes that the success of the NMCF 'will and must be measured in the happiness and welfare of our children, at once the most vulnerable citizens in any society and the greatest of our treasures.'

The NMCF is benefiting materially from purchases of this book, which will help to ensure that more of South Africa's children face a brighter tomorrow.

OPPOSITE: It was difficult to know who enjoyed Nelson Mandela's 79th birthday more — the President himself or the thousand or so children who gathered at the Culemborg Centre, Cape Town, in July, 1997, to help him celebrate it. In the carnival atmosphere the children, all suffering from life–threatening illnesses, watched spellbound as the President blew out the candles on his birthday cake, made in the shape of Table Mountain.

ABOVE: President Mandela joins the volunteers in the creative corner and tries his hand at some face painting with a willing young model. Looking on is Nelson Mandela Children's Fund chief executive trustee Jeremy Ractliffe.

❋ *Children*

THE
YOUNG ONES

LOUISE GUBB/i-AFRIKA

❋ 88   *Madiba*

Children

LEFT: A young girl gets close to Nelson Mandela on his visit to Nyanga, near Cape Town, in the run–up to the country's first all–race elections.

ABOVE: President Mandela meets one of the junior participants in a music competition at Athlone, near Cape Town.

Madiba 89

❋ Children

TIMES MEDIA LTD/GARTH LUMLEY

LOUISE GUBB/i-AFRIKA

❋ 90 *Madiba*

Children

OPPOSITE, TOP: A proud grandfather gets down to it with his grandson, Mbuso, at the Johannesburg nursery school which he attends.

OPPOSITE, BOTTOM: Pupils of King Edward School, Johannesburg, give their undivided attention to their future president.

ABOVE: The story teller... regaling pre-school children in Athlone, Cape Town.

LEFT: The centre of attraction at St Mary's High School, Johannesburg.

Madiba 91

❧ Children

JUDA NGWENYA

LOUISE GUBB/i-AFRIKA

ABOVE: Children present President Mandela with cars made from wire on the eve of his 77th birthday.

ABOVE, RIGHT: *Moses Leads His People* is the title of the book Nelson Mandela reads to children at their school in Soweto.

RIGHT: Children can never get too close to their President. If they can't be with him, they'll find a way to take him with them.

BENNY GOOL/SOUTHERN IMAGES

BENNY GOOL

❧ 92   *Madiba*

Children

COURTESY: MICHAEL JOSEPH

When Craig Joseph decided he would like to invite President Mandela to his Barmitzvah his family laughed at the idea, but Craig persisted and personally delivered an invitation to the President's home in Houghton, Johannesburg. Two weeks before the big event Mrs Cheryl Joseph was astonished to receive a call saying that if he had no other engagements the President would be delighted to attend.

Says Mrs Joseph: 'The 240 guests arrived and we ushered them into the hall and told them the President was arriving. They all smiled in disbelief — until he walked in. He was just awesome. He shook everyone by the hand and said to one guest, "You look exactly like Mr De Klerk". We did the *horah* to show him what a Barmitzvah was all about and he did his little *toyi–toyi* at the table.'

In his speech of welcome Craig told President Mandela: 'Your attendance at my celebration tonight makes this day even more special than I can describe. As a young Xhosa announces *Ndiyindoda* when he becomes a man, so I am celebrating the arrival of my manhood tonight. What a start you have given me to adulthood! It was a real dream of mine to have you come to my Barmitzvah. Tonight you have proven to me that dreams can come true. You have proven that many times over, to many people in South Africa and around the world. Your presence here tonight is further proof that you are not only a great leader, but a kind and caring person. Mr President, if you could arrange to lower the voting age to 13 you would definitely have my vote!'

ABOVE: A night to remember for (from left) Cheryl Joseph, Ricky Joseph, Craig Joseph and Michael Joseph.

Madiba

⚹ Children

LOUISE GUBB/i-AFRIKA

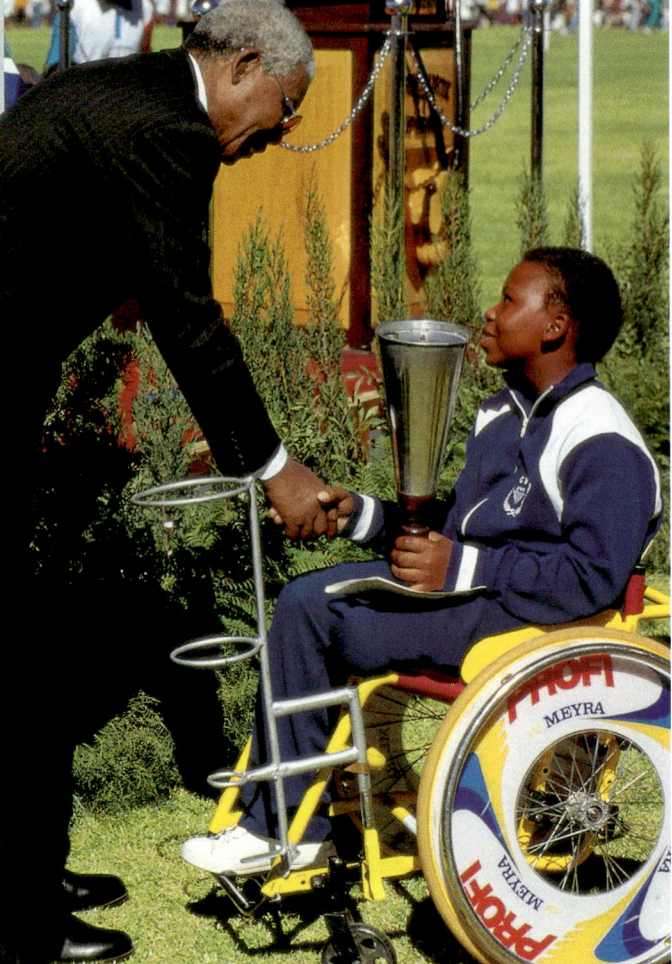

LOUISE GUBB/i-AFRIKA

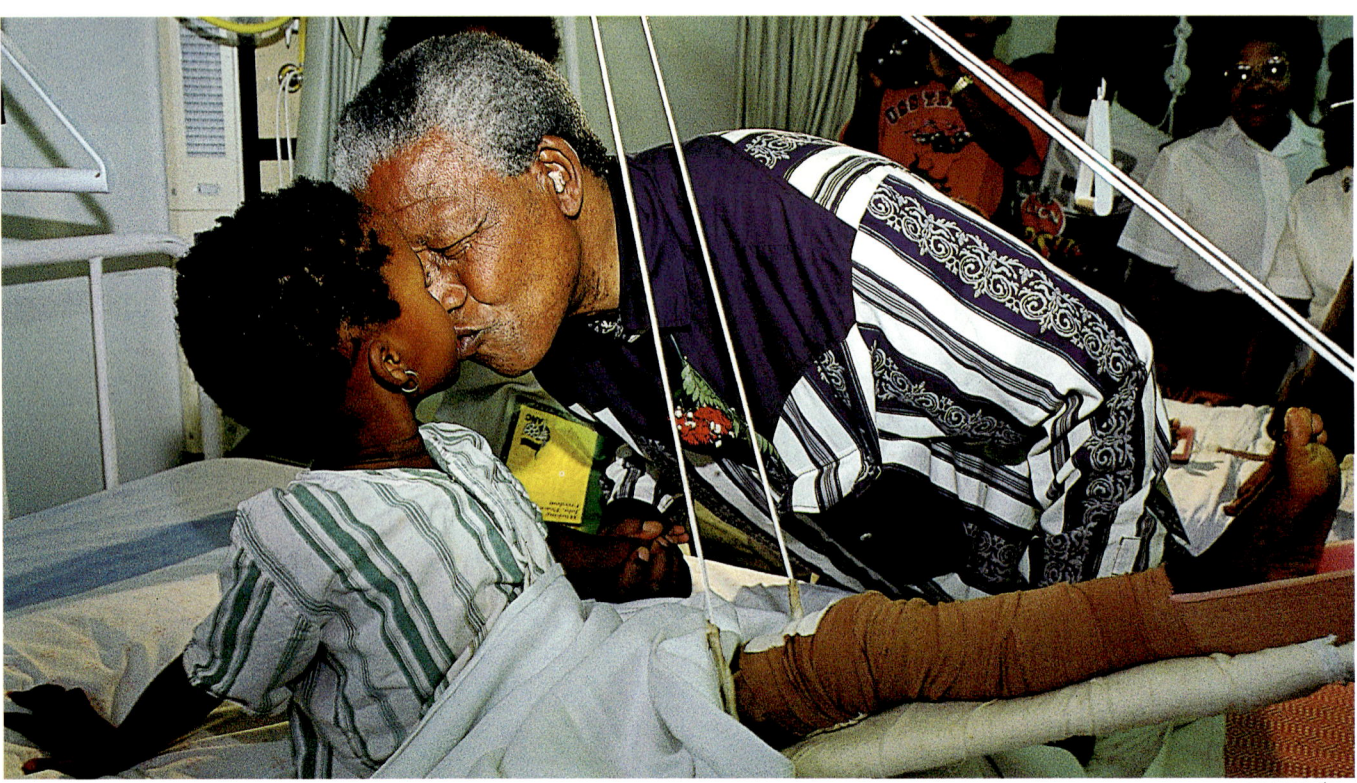

KEN OOSTERBROEK/ABPL

⚹ 94   *Madiba*

Children

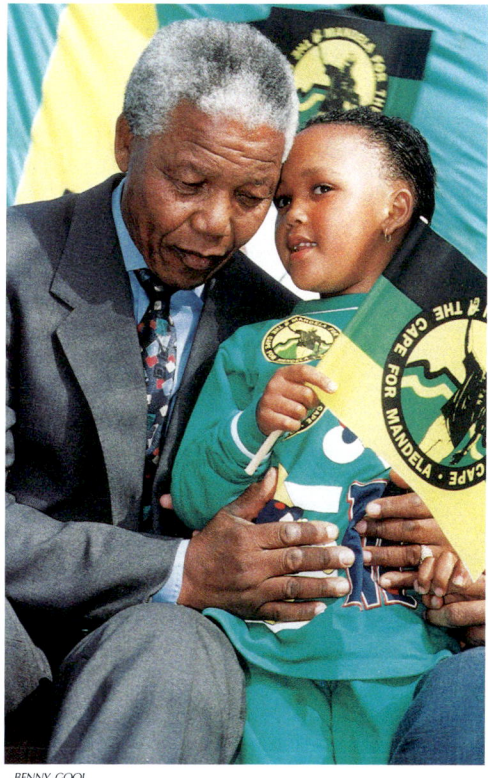

OPPOSITE AND ON THIS PAGE: Nelson Mandela has all the charm of an African Pied Piper for children from all walks of life.

Madiba

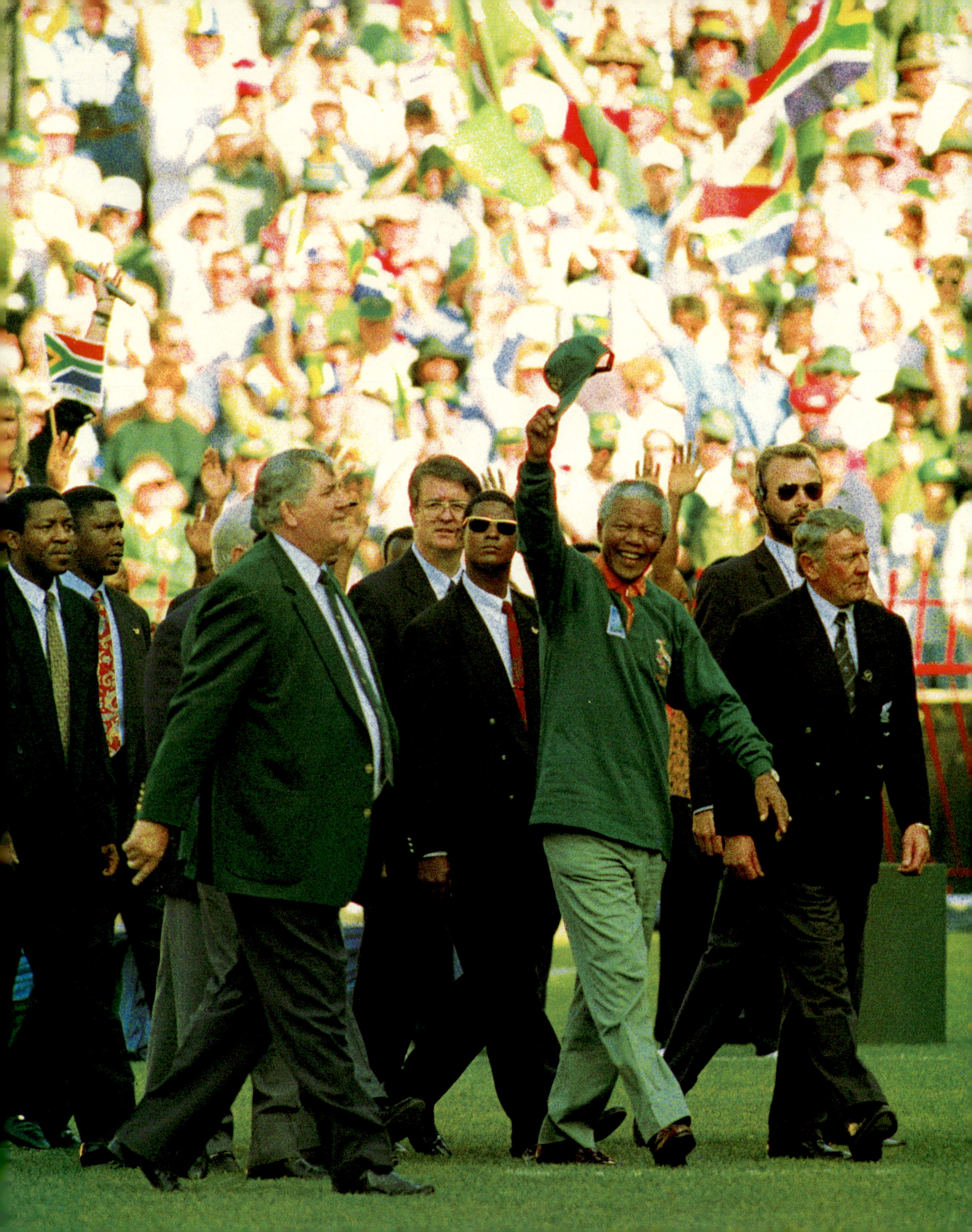

Talisman

THE MAGIC OF THE MAN

WESSEL OOSTHUIZEN/ABPL

President Mandela has become a talisman for South African sport. No one squeezed into Johannesburg's over–crowded Ellis Park Stadium will ever forget his Inauguration Day, May 10, 1994. A joyful crowd sang and cheered as South Africa's national soccer team, Bafana Bafana, played a match against Zambia. At half–time they cheered even louder when the new President, having travelled by helicopter from his inauguration ceremony in Pretoria, walked on to the field to meet the players and address his countrymen. South Africa had trailed 1–0 before his appearance. They played brilliantly in the second half to win 2–1 and

PAUL VELASCO/PICTURENET AFRICA

Madiba 97

⌘ Talisman

BOB GOSANI/BAILEY'S AFRICAN PHOTO ARCHIVES

From his earliest college days Nelson Mandela has been a keen boxer and a fan of the square ring. Even when facing the daily rigours of the drawn–out treason trial in Pretoria between 1958 and 1961, he went every evening after court to train at Jerry Moloi's boxing gymnasium in Johannesburg. After his training session Mandela would put in a late night stint at his city law office, where Transvaal flyweight champion Freddy *'Tomahawk'* Ngidi, spent his working days as an assistant.

ABOVE: Mandela squares up to Moloi for a sparring bout.

LEFT: President Mandela beams happily between former world champions Mike Tyson and Sugar Ray Leonard. Behind is boxing promotor Don King.

DAVID C TURNLEY/DETROIT FREE PRESS/COURTESY: AFRICAN NATIONAL CONGRESS ARCHIVES

Madiba

Talisman

scorer 'Doctor' Khumalo says he was inspired by the President.

Nelson Mandela recognised as a young man that there was more to sport than playing well. At Fort Hare University he played soccer and was a cross–country runner. He preferred running because, he says, lack of natural talent could be overcome by training and hard work. He became a keen boxer and wrote: 'I did not enjoy the violence of boxing as much as the science of it... how one used a strategy both to attack and retreat... in the ring, rank, age, colour and wealth are irrelevant.'

As a political leader Mandela has applied the lessons of those early boxing matches. With a skill worthy of Muhammad Ali in his heyday, Mandela has taken full advantage of the passion of so many South Africans for sport and used it as a unifying force for his young nation.

South Africa's participation in the 1992 Cricket

PREVIOUS PAGES: The game of rugby in South Africa has traditionally been a white man's sport. Imagine the fans' surprise when President Mandela walked onto the field at Ellis Park, Johannesburg, wearing the green and gold Number 6 jersey of national team captain Francois Pienaar at the 1995 Rugby World Cup final between South Africa and New Zealand.

LEFT: Gloved up again, the man who took the gloves off to fight apartheid.

BELOW: Taking tips from that maestro of the ring, former world heavyweight champion Muhammad Ali.

Madiba

⚘ Talisman

JAN HAMMAN

ABOVE: South African rugby captain Francois Pienaar receives his President's congratulations after the South African team defeated New Zealand 15–12 to win the 1995 Rugby World Cup and put the country firmly back on the world sporting map.

⚘ 100   *Madiba*

Talisman

World Cup, the first big international event in which South Africans competed after his release from prison, was the result of the Mandela magic.

Recalls Dr Ali Bacher, managing director of the United Cricket Board of South Africa: 'In July, 1991, we were readmitted into the International Cricket Council (ICC), the world controlling body of cricket, but were told that it would be premature for us to play in the World Cup in February, 1992. In August, 1991, I brought Clive Lloyd, the former West Indies cricket captain, to South Africa to coach black children in the townships and as a result of this I met Nelson Mandela for the first time.

'The media followed us into the meeting and when a reporter asked whether South Africa would be playing in the World Cup, President Mandela said, of course we must play. This was flashed around the world, the ICC reversed its decision, and we played in the World Cup. This gives an indication of his international clout. He is a brilliant strategic thinker and has seen that in South Africa the most important medium to bring together all races is sport, both on the field and off

TOP: Francois Pienaar deep in discussion with President Mandela, who developed such a good personal relationship with the rugby player that he invited him and his fiancé, Nerine, to lunch at his Pretoria residence to meet Graca Machel, and was guest of honour at Pienaar's wedding.

ABOVE: With former rugby supremo, Dr Danie Craven.

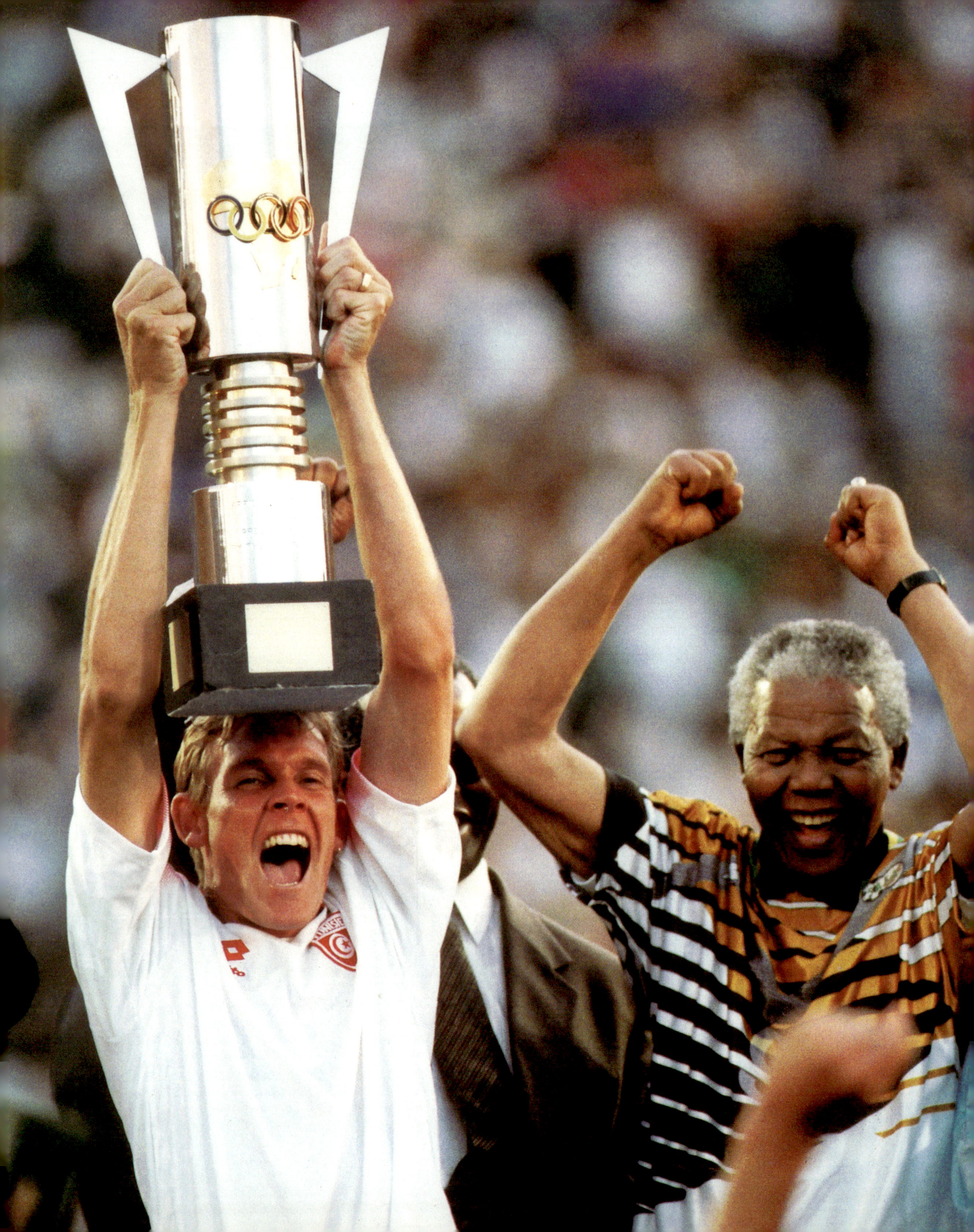

Talisman

the field. He is inspirational. The record shows that every time he has been to an international match we have won on every occasion, whether it be soccer, rugby or cricket. When the players know he is coming their performance is enhanced.'

There was concern about how the 1995 Rugby World Cup would be staged. Would it be a celebration of the new South Africa or the old? The answer came on a glorious opening day at the Newlands grounds in Cape Town. The stadium was a sea of brightly coloured new flags and when the President walked on, the crowd chanted 'Nelson, Nelson, Nelson'. When the anthems were played there was a surge of emotion and national pride, but as a unifying gesture, nothing matched the moment when President Mandela walked on the field wearing a Number 6 Springbok rugby jersey at the final at Ellis Park, Johannesburg. His delight in handing over the trophy to 'the other Number 6', Springbok rugby captain Francois Pienaar, was obvious and unrestrained and Pienaar added to the sense of euphoria and national well–being by saying his team felt the support of all 40 million South Africans.

Seven months later, President Mandela was guest of honour at South Africa's opening match against Cameroon in the African Nations Cup soccer tournament. With his side struggling at half–time, Bafana Bafana coach Clive Barker, told his men: 'That man spent 27 years in jail for you. Go out there and do something for him in 45 minutes.' They did and South Africa won 3–0. Bafana Bafana went on to reach the final where what had worked at the rugby final succeeded again. The President wore a replica of Bafana Bafana soccer captain Neil Tovey's Number 9 shirt. Again, the President handed over a trophy, the African Nations Cup, in front of an ecstatic, flag–waving crowd at the FNB Stadium, Johannesburg. Coach Barker's response was to take off his winner's medal and drape it around the President's neck, saying he felt the President had given so much of his time to motivating and inspiring Bafana Bafana that he deserved the medal as much as any of the players.

In sport, there is an old saying that even the greatest star is not as big as the sport he plays. The magic of Mandela is that in the eyes of the sportsmen and women he meets he is regarded as a legend bigger than sport itself. — COLIN BRYDEN, SPECIALIST SPORTS WRITER, SUNDAY TIMES.

PAUL VELASCO/PICTURENET AFRICA

OPPOSITE: Mandela is on hand to inspire South Africa again, this time watching the national soccer squad win the final in Johannesburg to carry off the African Nations Cup. Captain Neil Tovey shares the victory with President Mandela and recalls: 'The moment when I saw him coming on wearing my jersey will live in my memory for all time and one day my children and my grandchildren will relate to that moment of glory for the country and they will be able to say, "My father was there with the President". No one can take that away. When I was holding the cup he said to me, "You don't quite realise what you people have done for the country. Congratulations to you for your tremendous effort". I don't think he realises what a tremendous inspiration he is to all of us.'

ABOVE: The President in Neil Tovey's Number 9 shirt.

BELOW: Fêting South Africa's 1996 Olympic Games medallists, swimmers Marianne Kriel (left) and Penny Heyns (right) and marathon runner Josiah Tugwane. Not in this photograph is Hezekiel Sepeng who won a silver medal.

NAASHON ZALK/PICTURENET AFRICA

LEFT: JON HRUSA/ABPL

Talisman

ABOVE: Mandela is nothing if not an all–rounder. Here he poses with South African cricket captain Hansie Cronjé in Port Elizabeth after the national team beat England in the limited overs series to take the trophy in January 1996. Says Cronjé: 'My first meeting with President Mandela was in October, 1992, at Wanderers Stadium, Johannesburg, and what struck me was that he knew most of the players by name, and spoke to them in Afrikaans or English, depending on the person's home language. He has a magnificent relationship with sports people. He realises that they can play a major role in uniting South Africans and he has stressed that he fully supports us in whatever we do. He motivates us and makes us all proud to be South Africans.'

Talisman

BEELD

ABOVE: President Mandela with Dr Ali Bacher, managing director of the United Cricket Board of South Africa. Dr Bacher says as well as being an inspiration, the President is also a deeply caring person.
He remembers his wife receiving a telephone call from *Madiba* in 1993, at a time when few white South Africans knew who *Madiba* was. Mandela had heard that Dr Bacher was in hospital and was enquiring about his progress. 'I am told that's the norm with him. If he finds out that someone has lost a loved one or has problems of some sort he will phone them at any time of the day or night to find out how they are doing. He phoned another time and left a message to say the President had called. We thought it was the president of our cricket board, Kris Mackerdhuj, until President Mandela phoned again next morning. He wanted to see me for a discussion on why he had supported the Springbok emblem for rugby, while all the other national teams had opted for the Protea. With all the worldly calls on his time he invited me to lunch in Pretoria and spent an hour explaining why he went that route. It meant so much to him that we should be supportive of what he was doing. Clearly a caring person.'

Madiba 105

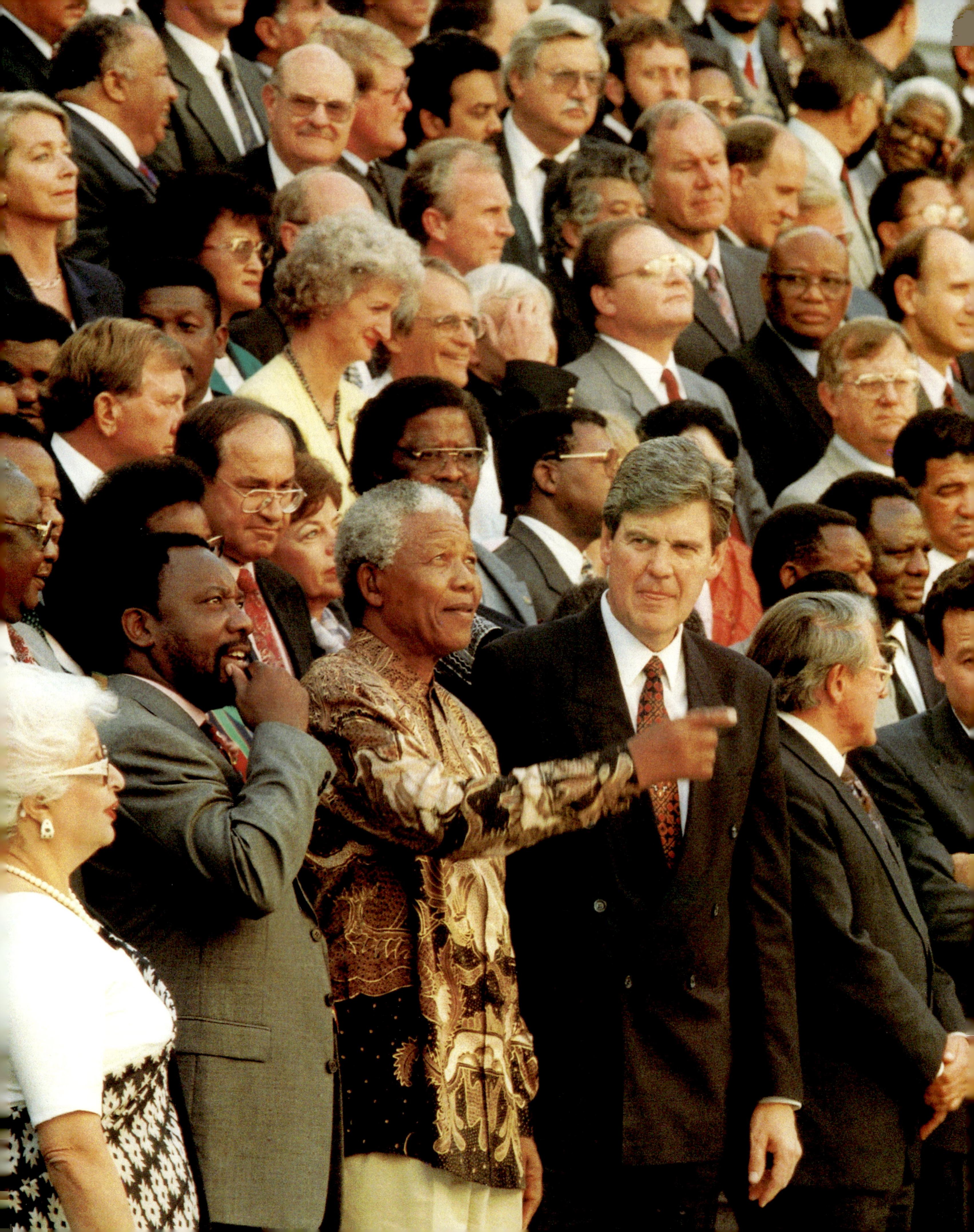

Style

THE DRESSER & THE DANCER

©KARINA TUROK AND ISLAND PICTURES

Nelson Mandela has led his young nation from the front, forgiving his jailers and those who jailed him, forging new friendships at home and abroad, inspiring the country's sportsmen and women to reach for the stars. But if there is one area in which his nation is loath to follow, then it is in the field of fashion. He wears, even on the most formal occasions, colourful, loose–fitting shirts, suggesting that perhaps his people should also adopt a more relaxed, informal, African style of dress. But here he is alone. The formal, Western style of dress continues to prevail in the establishment, and even his own cabinet ministers seem to prefer the stuffy collars, ties and suits that are an enduring legacy of imperial rule in Africa.

The President himself says simply: 'Everybody just looks at my face — not at my clothes', and confides that he finds it difficult to speak if he is wearing a bow–tie. He has also introduced a refreshing air of informality

LEFT: SASA KRALJ/I-AFRIKA

Madiba

Style

into the most formal of occasions by regularly breaking into a little dance — a kind of slow soft shoe shuffle — to express his delight at anything that takes his fancy. At that most solemn of public occasions, his official inauguration as President of South Africa, he delighted the crowds with his now–famous little jig, which has gained international currency as the *Madiba* Dance. It even had the Queen on her feet when the South African group Bayete performed it at the Prince's Trust Concert in London during July, 1996.

PREVIOUS PAGES: Standing out in the crowd (left) and (right) Mandela dances with delight as he listens to saxmen Peter Mokonotela and Thami Madi at a private party given for him by friends in Johannesburg during February, 1994.

Style

LOUISE GUBB/I-AFRIKA

LOUISE GUBB/I-AFRIKA

HENNER FRANKENFELD/PICTURENET AFRICA

LS M BOWEY – SA NAVY

Madiba 109

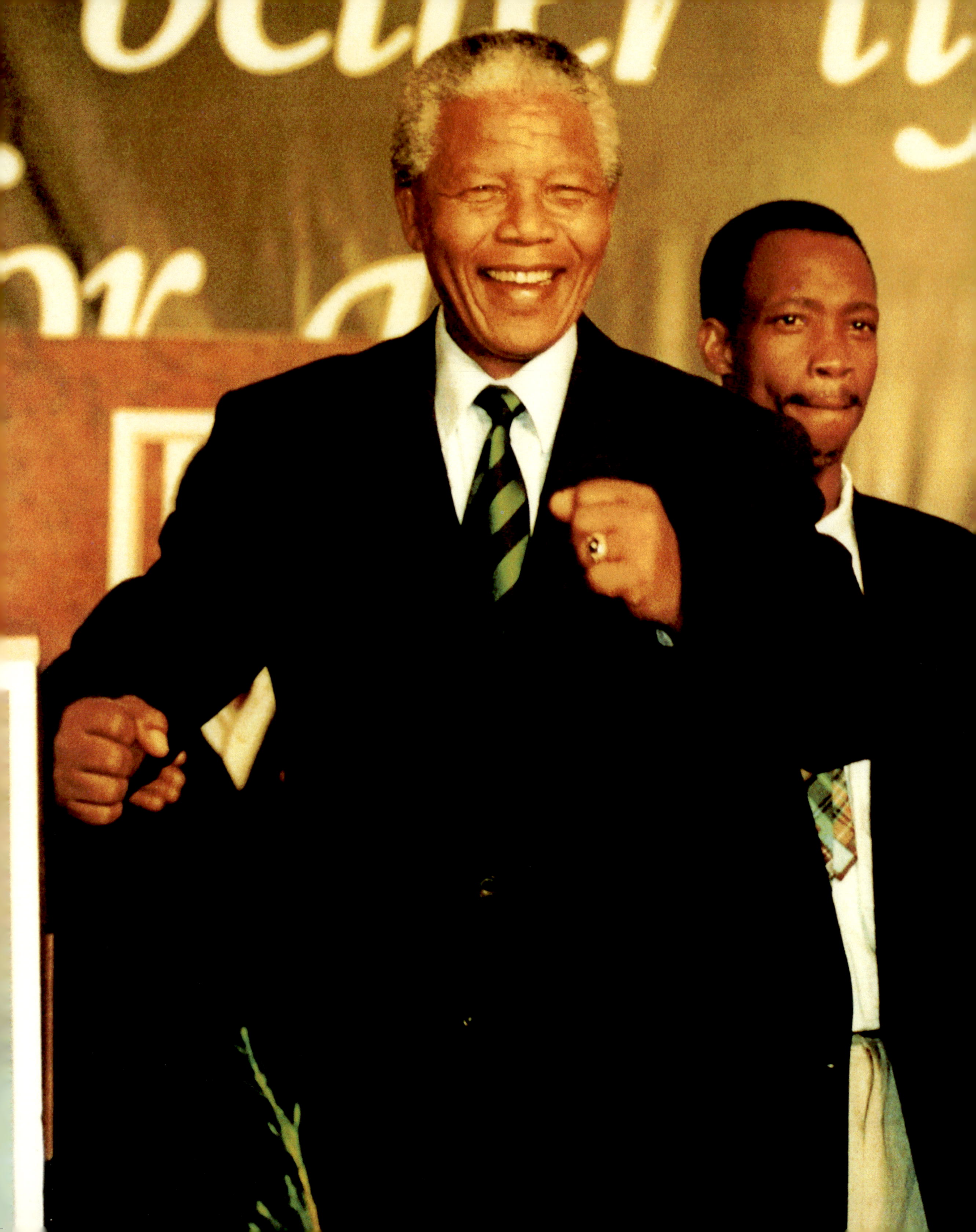

Style

SASA KRALJ/I-AFRIKA

GREG MARINOVICH/PICTURENET AFRICA

BENNY GOOL

LEFT: PAUL VELASCO/ABPL

Madiba 111

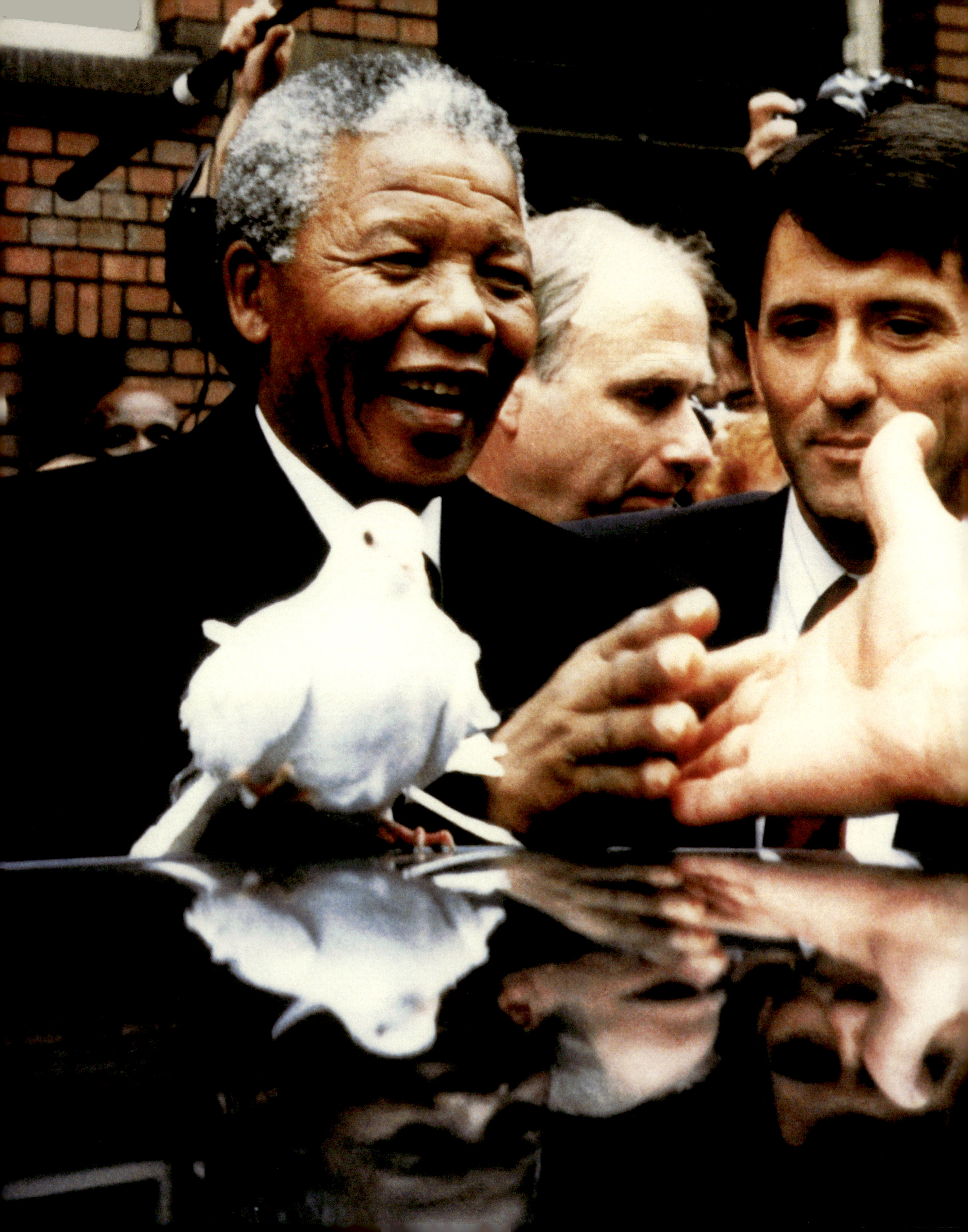

Spotlight

HELLO
WORLD

LOUISE GUBB/i-AFRIKA

If ever there was a man who has transcended his national boundaries and become in the true spirit of Renaissance Man a citizen of the world then that man is Nelson Mandela. After the almost mythical figure stepped out of muzzled confinement to become a live, flesh and blood person he has taken to the world and the world has taken to him. Both at home and abroad admirers from kings and queens, statesmen and religious leaders, to celebrities and pop stars have been proud to share the limelight with him.

OPPOSITE: A man of peace... Nelson Mandela extends the hand of friendship to the people of Amsterdam.

ABOVE: A gentle benediction from Pope John Paul II during his visit to South Africa.

↯ Spotlight

The texture of US–South African relations was fundamentally and irrevocably changed the day Nelson Mandela walked out of Victor Verster Prison, a free man. It was not only Mandela and his countrymen who breathed a sigh of relief when he was released; so did millions of Americans. It meant that, for the first time in nearly half a century, political and economic relationships between two countries whose people seem to have a natural affinity for each other could assume some semblance of normality.

Aside from official government–to–government relations, more Americans have known about, travelled to, worked in and argued about South Africa than any other country on the continent. While the two countries have much in common, their approaches diverged when they each turned in mid–century to deal with racial problems that could no longer be neglected. It is an interesting coincidence of history that as the US civil rights movement began to gather steam, South Africa moved in the opposite direction, expanding and entrenching official, government–sanctioned racial separation and discrimination; as Jackie Robinson broke the colour barrier in American professional baseball, Alan Paton was writing *Cry, the Beloved Country*; as the US Supreme Court was striking down segregated education, South Africa was passing Bantu Education and Separate Amenities Acts.

Resistance in both countries to racial discrimination accelerated in the 1960s. President John F. Kennedy's 'New Frontier' was forced to deal with increased pressure for equality as marches and demonstrations, riots and violence spread throughout America. Martin Luther King Jnr., pricked the conscience of America with his letters from Birmingham Jail and his 'I have a dream' speech at the nation's capital. America would never be the same.

In South Africa, resistance to apartheid sharpened in the wake of government repression, the massacre at Sharpeville and the founding of *Umkhonto weSizwe*. Within a few years of each other, Albert Luthuli and Martin Luther King Jnr., would receive Nobel Peace Prizes for their courageous stands against racial discrimination.

COURTESY: AFRICAN NATIONAL CONGRESS ARCHIVES

RIGHT: DAVID C. TURNLEY, DETROIT FREE PRESS/COURTESY: AFRICAN NATIONAL CONGRESS ARCHIVES

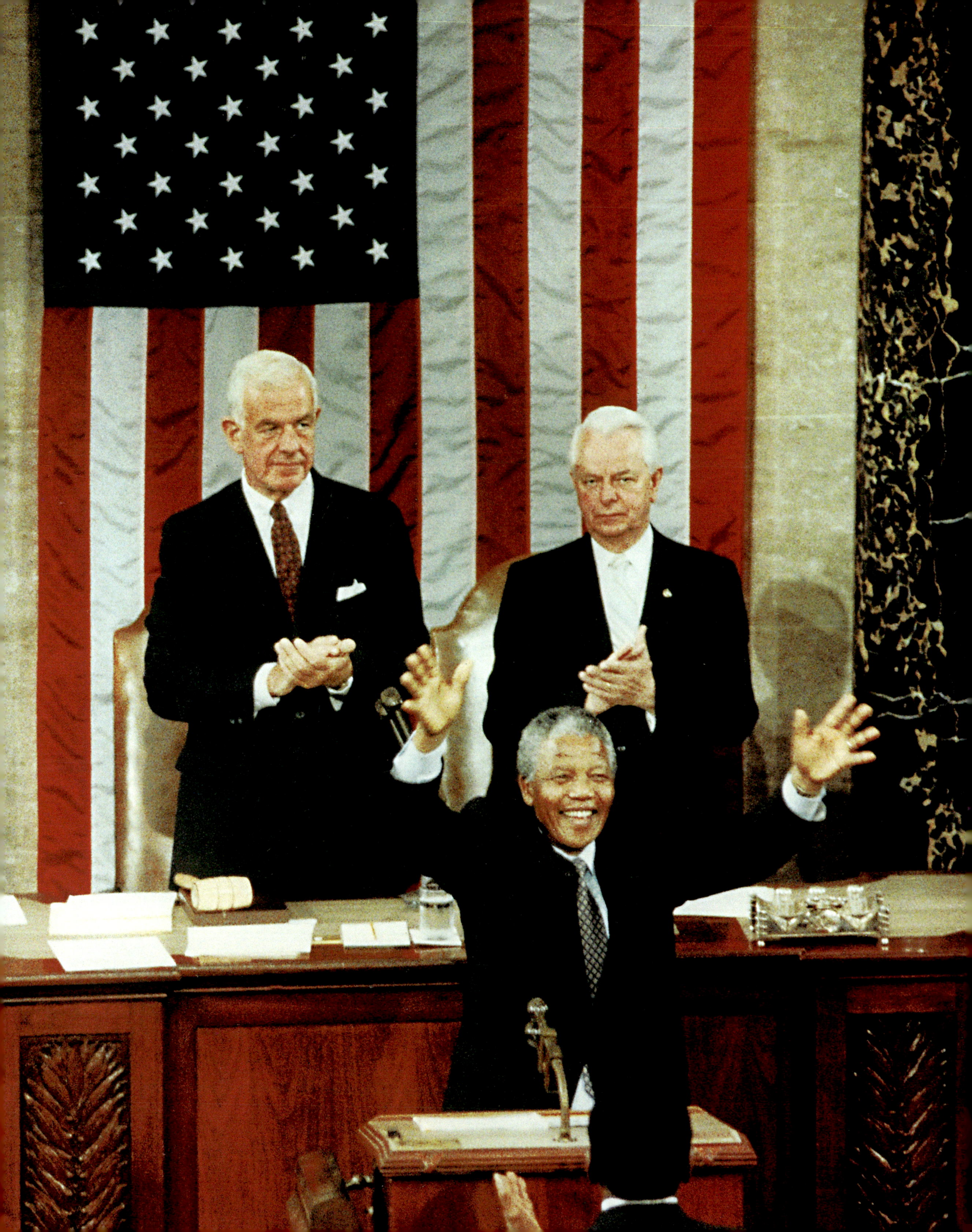

And Nelson Mandela's life imprisonment on Robben Island intensified the world's opposition and hatred of apartheid. South Africa, too, would never be the same.

For many in America, Nelson Mandela became the symbol of the struggle for freedom and justice in South Africa but the effort to demonise him as a terrorist and the ANC as a communist organisation was not without success.

America would become almost as deeply divided and troubled about South Africa, apartheid and Nelson Mandela, as it was about its own demons and racial fissures. South Africa's and America's tortured history of race relations became entwined, with the dispossessed in each country closely identifying with the other in their struggle for justice.

It is no wonder, then, that Americans reacted with such manifest joy to Nelson Mandela's release and his subsequent elevation to President in South Africa's first democratic elections. They had, in a sense, been a captive with him and experienced, with him, their own release.

It is undoubtedly the unique nature of the history of the US–South African relationship and the role that Nelson Mandela assumed in it that has given rise to the hero's reception he has been accorded in the US.

Few leaders are given the privilege of addressing a joint session of the US Congress. Nelson Mandela has done so twice. — GEORGE TRAIL, RETIRED US AMBASSADOR AND FORMER US CONSUL–GENERAL, JOHANNESBURG.

PREVIOUS PAGES: President Mandela takes to the floor with songstress Whitney Houston while President Bill Clinton (left) applauds, and Mandela makes an historic address to a joint session of the US Congress.

LEFT: Two presidents whose stature is the same in the democratic world, Nelson Mandela and Bill Clinton.

COURTESY: AFRICAN NATIONAL CONGRESS ARCHIVES

Spotlight

Left: Nelson Mandela draws a chuckle from US President George Bush during his visit to the US in June, 1990.

Below: US First Lady Hillary Clinton smiles as President Mandela makes his point during her visit to South Africa.

DAVID C TURNLEY, DETROIT FREE PRESS/COURTESY: AFRICAN NATIONAL CONGRESS ARCHIVES

LOUISE GUBB/i-AFRIKA

DAVID C TURNLEY, DETROIT FREE PRESS/COURTESY: AFRICAN NATIONAL CONGRESS ARCHIVES

Left and above: The widows of two famous American leaders meet an equally famous man from another continent — Coretta Scott King, widow of slain US civil rights activist Martin Luther King Jnr., and Mrs Jackie Onassis.

COURTESY: AFRICAN NATIONAL CONGRESS ARCHIVES

Madiba

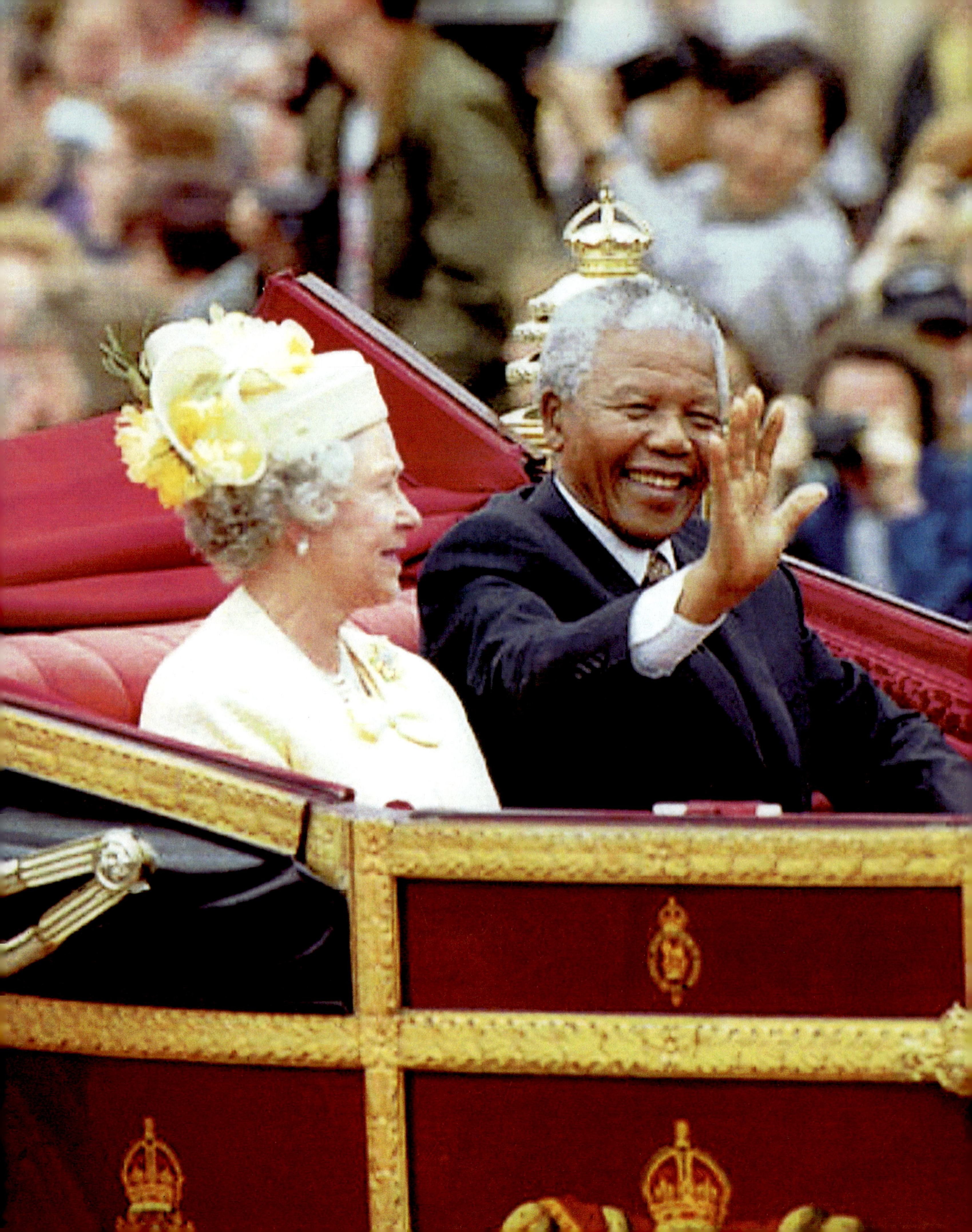

Spotlight

CROWNING GLORY

President Nelson Mandela happily confesses to being something of an Anglophile and has visited the United Kingdom on a number of occasions. The first time he was not received and fêted in the sceptred isle; he was operating underground and in London to collect the literature on guerrilla warfare that was forbidden in South Africa but deemed necessary to the advancement of the struggle for liberation.

Since his release from prison he has returned in triumph several times, to address the House of Commons at the Mother of Parliaments in Westminster as a suppliant in 1993, and as President of South Africa 1996, to ride in state with Queen Elizabeth II, and to visit then Prime Minister John Major at Number 10 Downing Street, and subsequently his successor, Tony Blair, in July, 1997.

John Major recalls one highlight of President Mandela's state visit as a guest of Queen Elizabeth in 1996: 'It is the only occasion I can recall where the staff of Number 10 — for whom the eminent of this world are standard fare — left their offices to line the corridors to applaud and welcome the President as he entered the house. Nelson may have thought this was routine, but it was not. Indeed, everywhere Nelson went during that visit he was surrounded by a warmth and respect from the British people which was a testament to the enormous affection in which he is held — not just by my own country, but around the world.'

A Buckingham Palace source says that President Mandela's friendship with the Queen is so close that he once wrote her a letter beginning 'Dear Elizabeth' and signed it simply, 'Nelson'. While this was a glaring breach of protocol, the Queen was not offended. Says the source: 'He is probably the only Head of State who could get away with that.'

Aside from the pomp and circumstance surrounding his latter visits, he found time within two months of his release from jail to address a rally at Wembley to thank the British people for their support of the African National Congress during the apartheid years and their unflagging efforts to secure his release from prison. He rose to say: 'Thank you that you chose to care, because you could have decided otherwise. Thank you that you elected not to forget, because our fate could have been a passing concern. We are here today because for almost three decades you sustained a campaign for the unconditional release of all South African political prisoners. We are here because you took the humane decision that you could not ignore the

LEFT: President Mandela is accorded the high honour of riding in state with Queen Elizabeth during his visit to Britain in 1996. The Queen cherishes a close friendship with South Africa's President, who visited at her personal invitation.

PICURENET AFRICA/ASSOCIATED PRESS

Madiba   119

⁌ Spotlight

inhumanity represented by the apartheid system.'

Like many other countries in Europe the British took Nelson Mandela to their hearts long before they saw him in the flesh, and from the far north of Scotland to the southern counties of England countless highways and byways have been renamed in his honour over the years. 'Free Mandela' pop concerts were regularly staged and drew thousands of chanting fans calling for the release of the man who went to jail for his beliefs before many of them were even born.

President Mandela thanked them all again when he told the United Kingdom's Joint Houses of Parliament in July, 1996: 'We take this opportunity once more to pay tribute to the millions of Britons who, through the years, and like others everywhere else in the world, stood up to say — no to apartheid. Our emancipation is their reward. We know that the freedom we enjoy is a richly textured gift hand–crafted by ordinary folk who would not allow that their own dignity as human beings should be insulted.'

— JIM PENRITH, FREELANCE WRITER, JOHANNESBURG

RIGHT: Standing in front of a portrait of one of Britain's greatest statesmen, Sir Winston Churchill, President Mandela clasps hands with John Major at the Prime Minister's official residence, Number 10 Downing Street.

BELOW: Normally unflappable British 'Bobbies' struggle to keep the excited crowd under control during President Mandela's visit to London.

LONDON PICTURE SERVICES/COURTESY: BRITISH INFORMATION SERVICES

PICTURENET AFRICA/ASSOCIATED PRESS

Spotlight

LOUISE GUBB/Î-AFRIKA

ABOVE: Queen Elizabeth with an attentive President Mandela after the unveiling in Soweto during her visit to South Africa in 1995, of a memorial commemorating the men of the South African Native Labour Corps who went down with the troopship *Mendi* in the English Channel during World War I.

Madiba 121

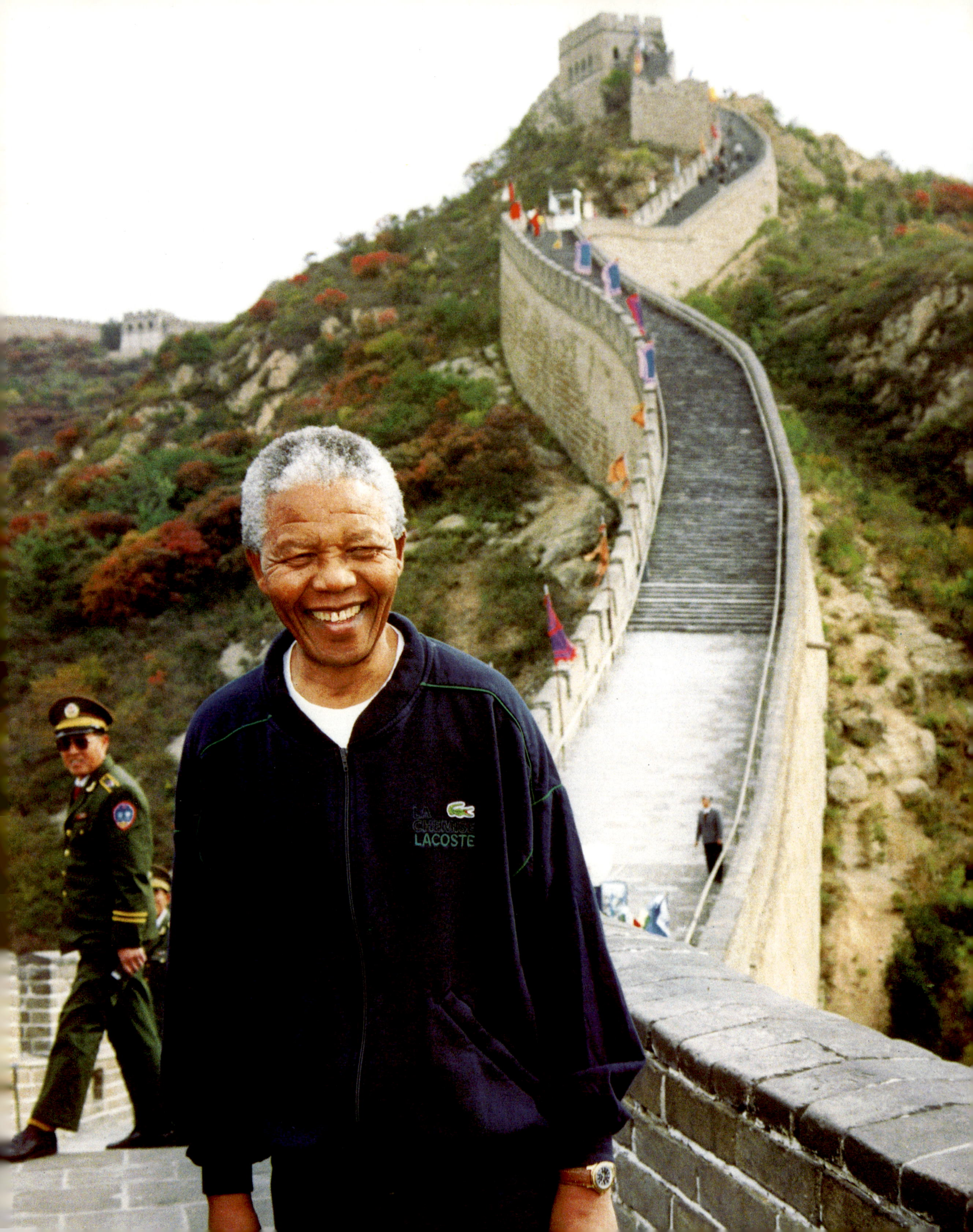
LA CHEMISE
LACOSTE

Spotlight

OPPOSITE: A beaming President Mandela takes a breather on the Great Wall during a visit to China.

LEFT: Honours galore have been heaped on President Mandela. Here he receives an honorary doctorate at the Sorbonne, Paris, in July, 1996.

BELOW LEFT: Arriving at the Malaysian parliament with King Sultan Tuanku Ja'afar Abdul Raman in March, 1997.

BELOW: Being escorted by Indian President Shankar Dayal Sharma in New Delhi, March, 1997.

Madiba

↳ Spotlight

↳ 124   Madiba

COURTESY: AFRICAN NATIONAL CONGRESS ARCHIVES

ERIC MILLER/i-AFRIKA

PICTURENET AFRICA/ASSOCIATED PRESS

OPPOSITE: Good neighbours... President Mandela with Namibian President Sam Nujoma (top) and (below) hosting African Heads of State in Cape Town during 1997. (From left) President Joaquim Chissano, Mozambique; President Quett Masire, Botswana; President Mandela; President Robert Mugabe, Zimbabwe; and President Yowere Musevene, Uganda.

ABOVE: With his strong moral authority, President Mandela has increasingly been drawn into African affairs as a peacemaker. In mid–1997 he shuttled between the South African Navy destroyer *SAS Outeniqua*, anchored off the coast of Zaire, and Cape Town, to mediate a resolution to the Zairean civil war, which saw Laurent Kabila (right) oust from power President Mobutu Sese Seko (left).

Madiba

※ Spotlight

ADIL BRADLOW/PICTURENET AFRICA

※ 126 *Madiba*

Spotlight

ERIC MILLER/i-AFRIKA

OPPOSITE: President Mandela lends American pop star Stevie Wonder a guiding hand during the blind singer's visit to South Africa.

ABOVE: A right royal joke convulses the President while Diana, Princess of Wales, seems to disclaim responsibility.

⇻ Spotlight

A man of irresistible charm... The ever-popular US film actress Whoopi Goldberg, and...

Spotlight

LOUISE GUBB/i-AFRIKA

...Miss Panama, an entrant in the 1996 Miss World contest held in South Africa. Both obviously agree that President Mandela is a man worth being close to.

Madiba

✤ Spotlight

THEY ALL COME TO MEET HIM — COMPUTER KINGS, COMEDIANS, POPULAR SINGERS, OPERA STARS AND SUPER MODELS.

ABOVE: Microsoft co–founder Bill Gates, the richest man in the world — all R166 billion worth of him — and the largest single donor to the Nelson Mandela Children's Fund, shares the spotlight with the world's most famous President.

TOP: Comedian Bill Cosby and his wife.

CENTRE: American pop star Paul Simon.

BOTTOM: World–famous Italian tenor Luciano Pavarotti.

Spotlight

COURTESY: NELSON MANDELA CHILDREN'S FUND/SALES HOUSE

ABOVE: Now hear this, says super model Naomi Campbell, who became the 50th member of the Nelson Mandela Children's Fund President's Club during her visit to South Africa, as well as a honorary granddaughter of the President.

Madiba

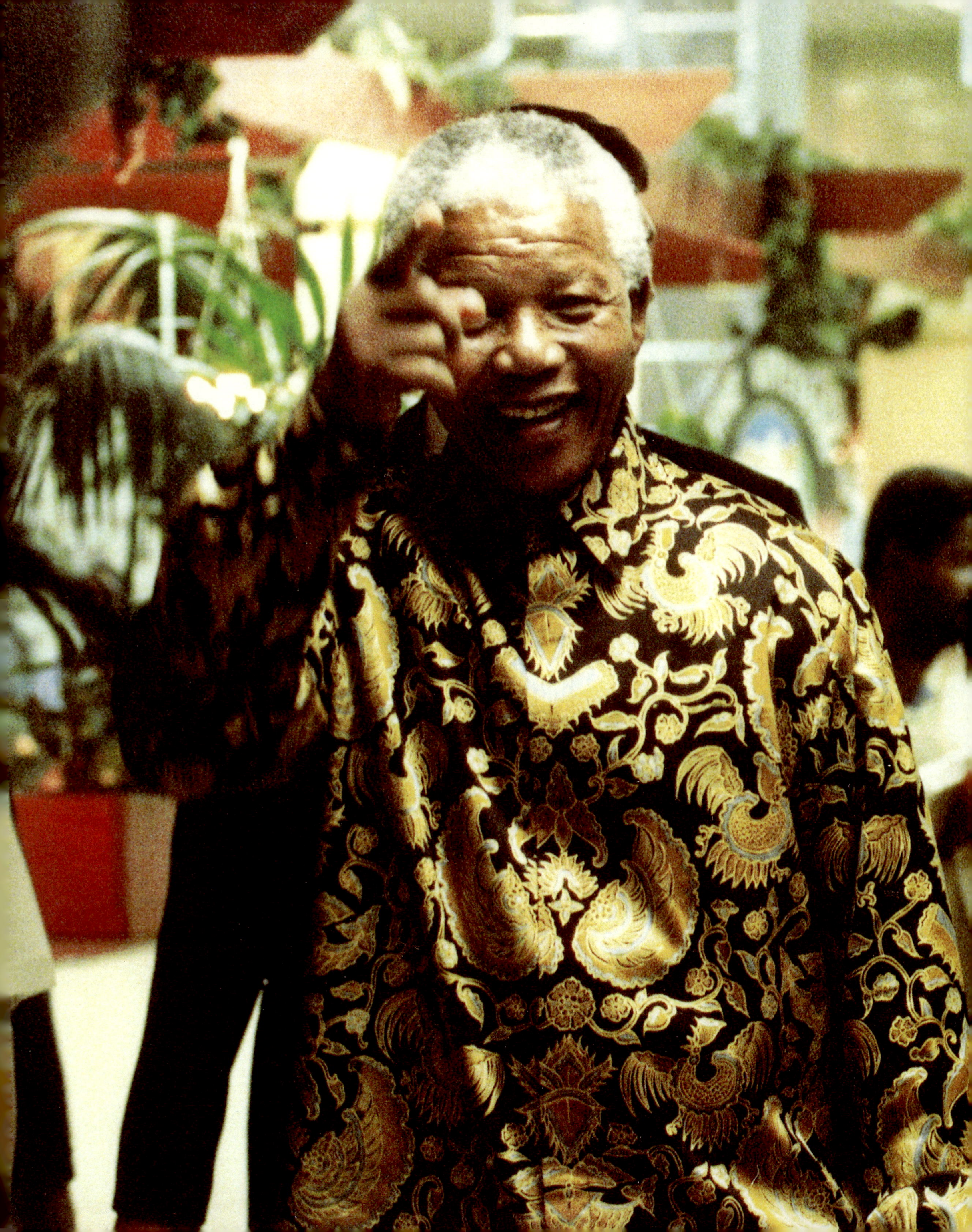

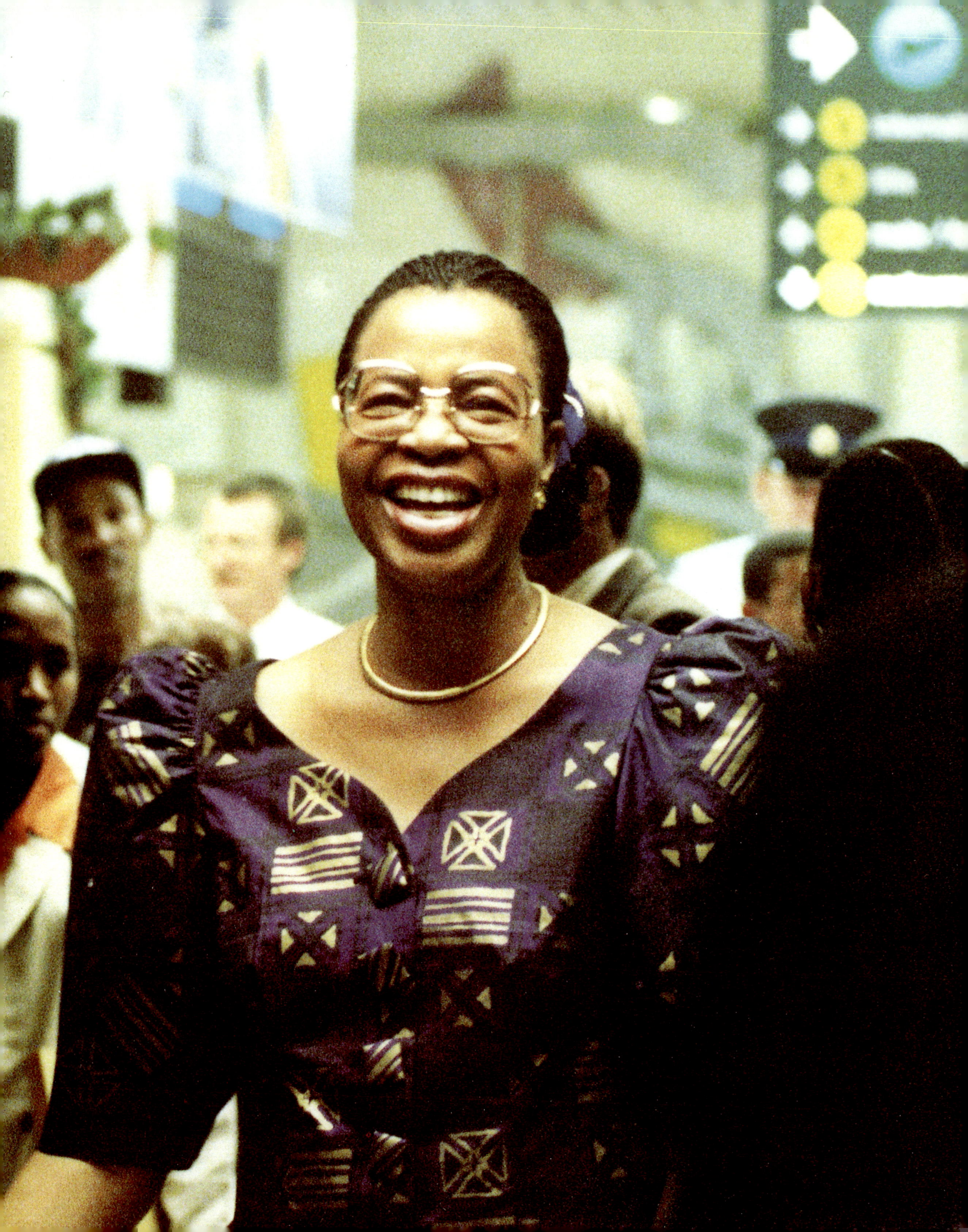

⊁ Companions

MAYIBUYE CENTRE

ONE FINE SPRING DAY

What South Africans had long suspected and conjectured about was made clear beyond all doubt when, one fine spring day in 1996, President Mandela and Graca Simbine Machel were for the first time spotted walking hand in hand in public around the leafy upmarket Johannesburg suburb of Houghton where the President has a private residence.

President Mandela had taken a fatherly interest in the widow of Mozambican president Samora Machel since the dying ANC leader Oliver Tambo had asked him to

MAYIBUYE CENTRE

⊁ 134   *Madiba*

LOUISE GUBB/I-AFRIKA

keep a protective eye on her and her children in recognition of Machel's past services and support for their organisation.

That this interest had deepened over the space of three years into a more romantic attachment had gradually become obvious, and the nation speculated on the future place of the woman who had become a close companion of the President and often accompanied him on State occasions. Lingering doubts about her position were dispelled when she moved into a house close to his own.

While some ANC supporters questioned through the columns of the press the wisdom of South Africa's Head of State partnering a non–South African citizen at official functions, the country by and large heaved a collective sigh of relief that President Mandela had found someone to cherish. As one close confidante says: 'After the trials and tribulations he has suffered, most people would like him to have a normal life and believe he deserves every little bit of happiness he can get.'

PREVIOUS PAGES: President Mandela and his constant companion, Graca Machel, caught in a happy mood while walking in the concourse at Johannesburg International Airport.
PHOTOGRAPH BY WALTER DHLADLA

OPPOSITE: Nelson Mandela with his first wife Evelyn (left) and (right) with second wife Winnie Nomzamo, who waited for more than 27 years for his release from jail. They separated barely two years after he was freed and the marriage ended in divorce.

ABOVE: Winnie Mandela keeps vigil during the long years alone.

Madiba 135

Companions

In his autobiography, *Long Walk to Freedom*, Nelson Mandela writes that '...with women I found I could let my hair down and confess to weaknesses and fears I would never reveal to another man'.

The first woman to share his innermost thoughts was Evelyn Mandela, the first wife he married when, as a young student of law, he was becoming an increasingly militant political activist in Johannesburg. The marriage collapsed under the rigours of his activism and terminated in divorce in 1958, leaving Evelyn with their two children, son Makgatho and daughter Makaziwe. Today Evelyn looks back on their life without rancour and says she chose the path of religion while Mandela chose politics, and this led to irreconcilable differences. 'We did not agree so we parted ways,' she says.

She now lives at *Cofimvaba* in Transkei, not far from Engcobo where she was born and which she left as a girl to complete her schooling and train as a nurse in Johannesburg. While in the City of Gold she stayed with her cousin, Walter Sisulu, and his family, where she met the young firebrand lawyer and politico who proposed marriage soon after meeting her and who recalls her in his autobiography as 'a quiet, pretty girl from the countryside'.

Shortly before filing for divorce Nelson Mandela was introduced by Oliver Tambo to a lovely young social worker. Her name was Nomzamo Winifred Madikizela, but she was better known as Winnie. Recalls President Mandela: 'I cannot say for certain if there is such a thing as love at first sight, but I do know that the moment I first glimpsed Winnie Nomzamo, I knew that I wanted to have her as my wife.' He married Winnie at a church in Bizana, her family home in Pondoland, on June 14, 1958.

Nomzamo turned out to be a prophetic name for the second Mrs Mandela. It means 'one who struggles or undergoes trials' and this is exactly what being married to a leading ANC activist meant, culminating a few short years after their marriage in the incarceration of Mandela and other ANC and *Umkhonto weSizwe* leaders on Robben Island to serve sentences of life0 imprisonment.

For the next 27 years their relationship consisted of occasional, brief visits and even more infrequent, censored letters. As the years passed Winnie became an internationally known figure as she moved centre stage in the ANC and suffered and survived persecution, scandals and controversy. What should have been a fairytale ending to her long wait

LOUISE GUBB/i-AFRIKA

GREG MARINOVICH/PICTURENET AFRICA

Companions

for the world's most famous political prisoner, petered out before the eyes of their bewildered supporters and admirers. Within two years of becoming the country's first democratically elected president, Nelson Mandela divorced his tempestuous wife after a four–year separation, undertaken because of what he described as 'tensions over a number of issues'.

Instead of nursing bitterness at being divorced by the husband for whom she had waited patiently for nearly three decades Winnie occupied her mind by helping what she regards as her real constituency: the homeless and the shack–dwellers. Of her headline–making divorce from the President in 1996, she says: 'It is painful, but much more painful for the children who waited 27 years to have a normal family life like other families.' There are two children of the marriage, daughters Zindzi and Zenani.

When the first reports of the president's affection for Graca Machel emerged one Sunday morning, Winnie was in a Johannesburg church with Zenani, son–in–law Prince Dlamini and grandchildren. Stormy petrel Winnie has consistently declined to comment publicly on the relationship and has instead involved herself more deeply in national and international affairs.

Graca Machel is described by those who have met her as charming and independent. She is also cultured and intellectual, and speaks English, Portuguese and French fluently. Graca Simbine was born in the southern Mozambican province of Gaza on October 19, 1945. After early schooling by Methodists she left Mozambique in 1967, to study for a university degree in languages in Lisbon. While there she became involved in politics and joined the Frelimo liberation movement. In October, 1973, Graca gained her degree and instead of returning to the Portuguese colony went to Tanzania where she underwent military training.

Her zeal resulted in her appointment as a teacher at Frelimo's high school at the Mozambique Institute in Dar–es–Salaam.

Graca went back to Mozambique a few days after the historic signing of the Lusaka Accord on September 7, 1974, which granted independence to the country. She was appointed Secretary of Education in the Frelimo–controlled Transitional Government, which ruled Mozambique until full independence in 1975. A month before her 30th birthday in 1975, she married Mozambique President Samora

PAUL VELASCO/ABPL

OPPOSITE TOP: Mandela and wife Winnie give the ANC power salute while walking in Archbishop Desmond Tutu's Cape Town garden the morning after his release from Victor Verster Prison.

OPPOSITE LEFT: In a room dominated by portraits of her ex–husband, Winnie Madikizela Mandela holds a media conference to announce her divorce from President Mandela.

ABOVE: Winnie and Nelson Mandela at a rally in Bloemfontein.

Madiba

Companions

Machel, who was a widower. In his cabinet she became Minister of Education and Culture and during her decade of stewardship the number of children enrolled at schools jumped from 400 000 to 1,5 million and she remains, to this day, one of the most popular figures in Mozambique.

Graca says she does not intend to marry President Mandela as that would make her a South African, and she has no intention of giving up her Mozambican nationality.
— ABBEY MAKOE, GAUTENG EDITOR OF DRUM MAGAZINE.

RIGHT: President Mandela pays silent tribute to the late President Samora Machel at the Mpumalanga site of the mysterious aircraft crash that took the Mozambican leader's life in 1986, and ended his long, supportive association with the ANC.

BELOW: Mandela and Graca Machel share a confidence.

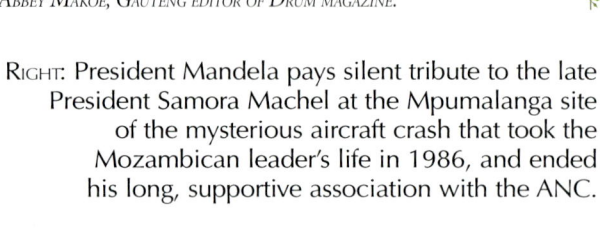

Companions

LEFT: The visit to South Africa of King Gustav of Sweden marked the first occasion on which Graca Machel accompanied President Mandela on official State business.

BELOW: The President and Graca with Archbishop Desmond Tutu.

Madiba

ANTON HAMMERL

HOME...

President Mandela now has elegant official residences in Pretoria and Cape Town but says he has always believed that a man should have a home within sight of where he was born. Although he was not born in the Transkei village of Qunu, it was where he spent his formative years, and he regards it as his home.

In 1993, he built a house there, identical to the one he lived in while in Victor Verster Prison, Paarl, which he says was the first spacious and comfortable home he had ever known.

Here, he returns whenever the pressures of state permit, surrounded by memories of his childhood, his extended clan family, and close to the grave of his mother, Nosekini Fanny, who died while he was in jail on Robben Island.

ANTON HAMMERL

140 *Madiba*

Home

ANTON HAMMERL

LOUISE GUBB/i-AFRIKA

OPPOSITE TOP: Bodyguards and photographers are hard–pressed to keep up with the sprightly President on his trek through the muddy rural areas surrounding the village.

OPPOSITE BOTTOM: A quiet moment as President Mandela looks through old books that have lain on this shelf since he left the village in his youth.

TOP LEFT: It is 4.30 am on Christmas Day, but it is not too early for *Madiba* to button up in preparation for his daily walk.

TOP RIGHT: President Mandela pays his respect at his mother's grave, who passed away while he was in jail.

LEFT: President Mandela points out the ruins of the hut he lived in after his family left his birthplace, Mvezo, to settle in Qunu.

ANTON HAMMERL

Madiba 141

↯ Home

GEORGE HALLETT

...FROM HOME

ABOVE: President Mandela in the lounge he calls the Elephant Room, at Genadendal, Cape Town. He has given this room a strong elephant motif, from the pictures on the wall to the curtain rod–ends holding the drapes.

RIGHT: With Priscilla Naidoo, public relations officer (left) and Zubeida Jaffer, a journalist and friend, in the Elephant Room.

GEORGE HALLETT

↯ 142 *Madiba*

Home

ABOVE: Housekeeper 'The Boss' Ella Govendor and Miriam Mngeni, put some final touches to the President's bedroom at Genadendal.

LEFT: The sunlit balcony of the Elephant Room facing Table Mountain is one of President Mandela's favourite places to relax.

Madiba

Acknowledgements

The publishers wish to express their appreciation to President Nelson Rolihlahla Mandela, who gave his blessing to this publication in his capacity as chairperson and founder of the Nelson Mandela Children's Fund, which will benefit materially from purchases of this book. Jeremy Ractliffe, chief executive trustee of the Nelson Mandela Children's Fund, Maeline Engelbrecht, and other members of his staff rendered invaluable assistance.

Equally invaluable was the contribution of Vodacom, which made publication of this book possible by providing substantial support.

This book is dedicated to the children of South Africa and to the memory of Kate Vere–Davies and her sons, Luke (10) and James (4). Kate, who was our principal picture researcher, and Luke and James died in a motor accident during the last stages of this book's production. For many months before her tragic death, Kate had dedicated a vast amount of her boundless energy to a tireless quest for the best photographs of President Mandela.

Another special person who has made an important contribution to this book is the Most Reverend Desmond M Tutu, Archbishop Emeritus and Chairperson of the Truth and Reconciliation Commission. Despite the great spiritual, emotional and physical demands made upon him, he responded graciously to our request to contribute the foreword.

Others who gave of their expertise and time include:
Former British Prime Minister John Major; Baroness Lynda Chalker;
Prof Peter Mtuze, Department of African Languages, Rhodes University;
Dr Ali Bacher, managing director, United Cricket Board;
Hansie Cronjé, captain of the South African cricket team;
Neil Tovey, former captain of Bafana Bafana, the national soccer team;
John Winter, curator, Kirstenbosch National Botanical Garden, Cape Town;
Graham Goddard, Mayibuye Centre, Cape Town; John Allen, Director, Media Liaison, Truth and Reconciliation Commission; Lavinia Browne, personal assistant to Archbishop DM Tutu; Ingrid Uys, specialist writer, Cape Town; Dr Percy Amoils; Amina Cachalia; Beryl Baker, African National Congress; Santa Baasch, stills, and Kenny Miller, graphics, SABC TV News Graphics; Rodney Hartman, Sports Editor, Sunday Times; Dick Foxton; Ahmed Kathrada; Helmut and Ruth Greiter; Helmut and Veda Schneider; Cheryl Joseph; Dr Numuyo Nokwe, Harry Schwarz and Nancy Ncube.

Publication of a pictorial book would, of course, not be possible without the co–operation of photographers. Many of South Africa's finest photographers dug deep into their archives to find the memorable images reproduced in the pages of this book. Wherever possible, we have acknowledged photographers by noting their names next to their photographs. Some photographs presented to President Mandela and made available to us by the African National Congress did not bear the names of photographers.
We regret that we have not been able to formally acknowledge their contributions.

Writers who contributed to this book made a special effort to capture the spirit of President Mandela. We thank them, and we also acknowledge that Shaun Johnson, Group Editorial Director of Independent Newspapers of South Africa, has requested that the fee for his keynote feature, *The Mark of the Man,* should be ceded to the Nelson Mandela Children's Fund.

COURTESY: AFRICAN NATIONAL CONGRESS ARCHIVES

At the end of his long walk to freedom Nelson Mandela will hand over the reins of the presidency in 1999, to enjoy a well–earned rest. Deputy President Thabo Mbeki (above) is seen as a likely successor, but whoever takes over will find it a hard act to follow...